Notting Hill Editions is an independent British publisher. The company was founded by Tom Kremer (1930–2017), champion of innovation and the man responsible for popularising the Rubik's Cube.

After a successful business career in toy invention Tom decided, at the age of eighty, to fulfil his passion for literature. In a fast-moving digital world Tom's aim was to revive the art of the essay, and to create exceptionally beautiful books that would be cherished.

Hailed as 'the shape of things to come', the family-run press brings to print the most surprising thinkers of past and present. In an era of information-overload, these collectible pocket-size books distil ideas that linger in the mind.

Duncan Minshull is a freelance audio producer and anthologist. His publications include the bestselling *Beneath My Feet: Writers on Walking* and *Sauntering: Writers Walk Europe* (both Notting Hill Editions); as well as *While Wandering* (Vintage) and *Where My Feet Fall* (William Collins). He has written about the joys of walking for *The Times*, the *Financial Times*, the *Guardian*, the *Telegraph*, *Condé Nast Traveller*, *Vogue* and *Psychologies*. And he takes people for 'walk and talks' in various parts of the UK.

GLOBETROTTING
Writers Walk the World

–

Introduced and edited by
Duncan Minshull

nh Notting Hill Editions

Published in 2024
by Notting Hill Editions Ltd
Mirefoot, Burneside, Kendal, LA8 9AB

Series design by FLOK Design, Berlin, Germany
Cover design by Tom Etherington
Creative Advisor: Dennis PAPHITIS

Typeset by CB Editions, London
Printed and bound by Imak Ofset, Istanbul, Turkey

Cover photograph: Laura Gilpin (1891–1979), 'Foot Prints in the Sand.'
1930s; Platinum print; reproduced with kind permission of the Amon
Carter Museum of American Art, Ft Worth, Texas, Bequest of the
Artist; P1979.123.115.

Introduction copyright © 2024 by Duncan Minshull

A CIP record for this book is available from the British Library

ISBN 978-1-912559-45-9

nottinghilleditions.com

Sit as little as possible.

– Friedrich Nietszche

There was nowhere to go but everywhere.

– Jack Kerouac

Contents

PART TWO: EN ROUTE

DUNCAN MINSHULL

– Introduction –

I n a volume preceding this one (called *Sauntering: Writers Walk Europe*), Théophile Gautier wandered the ancient cemetery of Pera, Istanbul, and slowed by a tomb 'diapered with azure and gold'. Here, he told us, he might light a 'chibouque', have a coffee, and gaze awhile . . . and so ended his rather short walking story, caught in a hundred footsteps, or less.

But it's tempting to think what lay behind the writer's gaze, related to things pedestrian. Was it not a gaze beyond the walls of Pera to points farther flung? To footsteps across other parts of Europe. Across Africa and Asia, the Americas and Antarctica, and Australasia too. Footsteps across all sorts of land and cityscapes, in all sorts of climes and times; be they solitary, paired, or grouped. Footsteps that suggest a host of reasons for leaving the sedentary life behind.

If Gautier's thoughts were not expansive, were just about having a smoke in the 'weird moonlight' of a certain spot, then fine: let's leave him there . . . loitering. But an attempt has been made to find the farther points, and they form the pages of the book you hold: *Globetrotting: Writers Walk the World.* The first are planted by the banks of the River Thames, and the last are laid down in a suburb of Melbourne – yes, there are many, *many* footsteps to come. Their trajectories are caught in extracts from essays and letters, diaries and memoirs. Plus, the rhythm of walking gets us singing on occasion, so expect a sprinkling of songs within earshot. It's almost sixty journeys done!

Which meant this editor's first task was to guide them towards a direction of travel; towards a narrative shape. Allowing you, the walker reader (for I'm betting you walk as much as you read), to make your way through three sections familiarly trod. At least you know where you are with the promise of 'Setting Off', the joys of being 'En Route', and the fatigue of 'Final Steps'. And according to some writers, the world's seven continents wait to be 'strolled' and 'scampered', 'roamed and 'rambled', 'tramped' and 'trotted' in the sections mentioned. I began with Europe, put Africa second, Asia third, and so forth, to show how our footsteps move across contrasting ground; in the heat, the cold, and the temperate; in 1492 and in 2010 – as a searcher of the New World steps upon Bird Rock, Bahamas, 'wandering for good water', beguiled by the wildlife; and as a more recent figure records a different kind of wildlife – a human, urban one – on the streets of pre-war Kyiv.

It's actually mid-collection when Thomas Jefferson asks the question any walker reader would ask: *why* do we walk?

He provides a reasonable and limited answer – for fresh air and exercise; ah, leaving the desk and taking to the road is good for everyone. But if a message is due, it's that wherever the road leads, fresh air and exercise are only the tip of it. Early in 'Setting Off', barely into full stride, we learn how the world opens up on foot; and as we pass through it, our senses become sharpened. Aiming, say, for the 'tip-top' of Table Mountain, the sights are far-ranging (Cape Town stretching below) and near to (the little bits of leather from long abandoned boots). And somewhere else entirely: hear the sounds on the breeze: the chants of coffee-bean carriers as they lug loads around Rio de Janeiro. Old chants to clear the streets of the traffic – of the dawdlers and the dalliers, and the newly arrived.

Sights and sounds; and a smell and a touch (the 'scent' of sugar trees, the 'chill' of late night, in remote Japan). And as the senses soar, so does the mental side of walking intensify. In 'Setting Off', we witness how physical movement frees the mind to wander; often brightly, to those farther points. Heading north from the aforementioned Thames, a stranger describes how life on the thoroughfare overwhelms him; how this 'human Niagara' carries along all shapes and hues imaginable. Who are the people of the pavements? he asks aloud, slowing to a halt, taking stock, and his confusion turns to awe eventually.

Another time in 'Setting Off', it's to the polar regions: to where a small group ponders the big whiteness, prior to leaving camp to map out the territories. And to be engulfed, they conclude. But the trek will imbue each man with a sense of comradeship in extremis; as if walking as *one* into the whiteness . . .

into a state of equanimity . . . into a state of collective well-being. The leader of the group observes this special 'spirit' emerging: 'If anyone thinks Wisting, Hassel, and Bjaaland took a solemn farewell from of us who stayed behind – no. They left the tents at 2.30 a.m., and vanished in their directions amid much laughter and chaff together!'

That leader was Roald Amundsen, the first to reach both poles, who traverses the sections ahead with a number of fellow explorers and adventurers. They cross the snows and the sands, and climb the peaks, for a variety of reasons: to claim land for self or nation, to find new species, to settle old scores (and regarding the last, you'll meet a 'fine figure of a man in sombrero and leggings', admired by the hobo-ette, Ethel Lynn). They make their locations on foot of course, because whatever the age, an animal or an engine only gets you so far – then the real story begins. And don't they know how fitting, how heroic, it can be to travel like this, even if plain necessity is the driver.

The more I guided people into *Globetrotting*, the more I found they spoke as types. Why walk, and *who* walks? Yes, there are the explorers and adventurers, with specific aims and routes; and there is someone quite the opposite – quite the polar opposite – who doesn't hike or climb or wade. He or she is the stroller. Out and about in the name of curiosity and quirky quest. Where the walk itself becomes a creative act, the subject matter committed to the page. Théophile

Gautier was one of these types; and soon Mark Twain, observing the antics of a 'dandy' in Geneva, and Edith Wharton, attuned to the moods of after-hours Fez. And it is Michèle Roberts strolling deeper into the 'blue dusk' of Kyiv – a merry, saucy, bold Kyiv – as she seeks the spirit of its historic protector, Saint Olga.

'Let's go . . . somewhere', says D. H. Lawrence in 'En Route'. He duly 'strays' for miles in rural Mexico with his wife Frieda; amused to be seen as 'potential brigands' by passers-by and content not to find 'fresh frutas' immediately, so the quest can continue into late afternoon. The novelistic eye is keen ('Rosalino's pink tongue swelled out his throat like a cobra'), ditto the ear ('the deep, musical volley of *Adios*!'); and on such a baking Sunday as this, the journey reveals an enticing truth to the two super strollers: you should wander at ease, and live in the moment looking for oranges, because 'the next five minutes are far enough away'.

The world is a Niagara of these types – the sightseers and the fun lovers – ambling in all eras across piazzas and gardens and waterfronts; and there's lots of fun in following them. But it's inevitable that for every Twain, Wharton, and Lawrence (and every Herman Melville, Franz Kessell and Mrs Coopland), other figures have taken a dark and dangerous turn. What is more, they had little choice but to go this way.

The world is also a Niagara of paraders, and pageanteers, and marchers, claiming the streets in celebration, in agitation, – or worse. For only suffering sends a mass of men, women, and children towards the Narva

Gate in Moscow, singing 'Hurrah . . . God Save Thy People . . . Death or Freedom'. And history repeats itself, decades on, same city, as larger crowds are seen to 'shuffle' past the sarcophagus of a dictator bathed in brilliant light; more muted this time, but exuding the Narva gloom and disquiet. Again, the people are walking to what exactly? What kind of destiny?

On a different continent, North America, the Northern Star burns brightly overhead. Fixed and friendly-looking for any adventurer or mapper to plot a course by. But the star guides another traveller: one with little choice but to flee the deep south for the urban north. Which involves 'walking by night, hiding by day', with repeated rendition of the Promised Land to keep all hopes alive. It is Harriet Tubman proceeding so; a 'runaway slave' and renowned social activist in later years. Likewise, Molly, Daisy and Gracie dart amongst the dunes and woods of Western Australia, runaways from the confines and cruelties of the government settlements. The girls proceed to track their own lodestar – row upon row of rabbit-proof fence – in order to find a spot that will suggest safety.

And what the reader will find in such accounts is something remarkable. Here the protest march and the escape are acts of desperation. Any thoughts on, or delights in, the walk are irrelevant, as only results matter. But the hard miles covered in Moscow, the Deep South, and western Australia, do recall *other* aspects: a growing kinship, an affinity with environment, and, in the girls' case, an eye for the fantastical out there – was

it really a 'marbu'? asks Molly. She refers to the creature from the Dreamtime, thudding along the trail . . .
better hide behind a banksia tree!

The 'marbu' is a figment of Molly's imagination. But
he's still one guided into *Globetrotting* who belies an
obvious type, and long may he thud. Outlier and often
singular, you'll see others like him – somewhere. Perhaps Paris, where the streets are roamed at night by a
figure re-cast as 'vagabond'. In this guise he is unbound,
an onlooker of everything the city has to offer, refined
and depraved. At night, in a forest clearing in Ghana,
another one drinks, paces his veranda, and if he can't
make out the floorboards, knows it's time to hit the
sack – 'the lonely man's walk', he admits, with a smile.
Whilst Julia Pardoe decides she has to join a chain of
'jog-trotters', heading to a rather strange ceremony,
at a point close to midnight, in the Belém suburb of
Lisbon.

The vagabond, the lonely man, and Julia Pardoe.
Each navigates the darkness alone. Which in certain
parts of the world is truly singular; though worth it.
In places lamplit, or half lit, or unlit, the senses have
to re-adjust: the sights are strangely rendered, even the
familiar ones, and the sounds accentuated, carrying far
on the night air. The nocturnal walker reacts differently
as well: is charmed and mystified; maybe lost, maybe
fearful. The hours of transformation surely enthral this
trio. As do similar hours for Raja Shehadeh on the hills
of A'yn Qenya, Palestine; and Rabindranath Tagore on

the sands of coastal Bengal; and Isabella Bird in the distant town of Lebungé, Japan.

And in 'Final Steps', in the twilight too, historian and adventurer, Alexander Kingslake, climbs a plateau to gaze back and consider his wanderings through the dusty quarters of Asia. There's little of the laughter and chaff experienced in those other, whiter wastes, but you sense the contented fatigue here. It's a fine moment to come to a halt:

I used to walk towards the East, confiding in the print of my foot as a guide for my return . . . But wherever we wander, we still remain tethered by the chain that links us to our kind; and so I began to return – to return, as it were, to my own gate . . . reaching high ground at last, I could see with delight, the fire of our small encampment. The Arabs were busy with their bread; Mysseri was rattling the cups; and two or three yards from the fire my tent stood prim and tight with its open portal and welcoming look – a look like 'the own armchair' of our lyrist's 'sweet Lady Anne.'

And I hope, reader walker *you* will find an armchair in a certain spot, have a coffee and a chibouque (it's a pipe of sorts), and follow these many, many footsteps. Made by compelling types. Across the seven continents. In the daylight and the darkness. Then, who knows, some of the stories told might just persuade you to open a gate and get going somewhere in the world . . . after a while, that is.

Happy reading. And trotting.

Setting Out on Seven Continents

I have to report that one fine morning the desire to
take a walk came over me.

— Robert Walser

– What a World was Seen Afoot! –

S kiffs from the shore pulled alongside, and after a little quarrelling, we were deposited in one, with a party who desired to be landed at the Tower Stairs. The dark walls frowned above us as we disembarked from the water and walked to an open square on the outside of the moat. The laborers were about commencing work, and there was noise and bustle in the streets, particularly when we set off to Whitechapel, part of the great thoroughfare, extending through the heart of London to Westminster Abbey and the Parliament buildings. Further on, through Leadenhall Street, Fleet Street and the Strand – and what a world was seen afoot!

Here come the ever-thronging, ever-rolling waves of life, pressing and whirling in their tumultuous career. Here, day and night, pours the stream of human beings, seeming amid the roar and din and clatter of the passing vehicles, like the tide of some great combat. How lonely it makes one to stand still for a moment, and feel that of all the strollers which divide around him, not one of them knows or cares for him. And what does he know of the thousands who pass him by? How many bearing the impress of god-like virtue, or hiding beneath a goodly countenance, have a black heart of crime? How many fiery spirits, all glowing with hope for the yet unclouded future, are brooding over a darkened and desolate past in an agony of despair? There is a sublimity in this human Niagara that makes one look at his own race with something of awe.

From *Views Afoot, Or, Europe Seen with Knapsack and Staff*, 1852

LADY ANNE BARNARD

– Old Soles –

I t is 3,500 feet in height, and reckoned three miles to the top from the beginnings of the ascent; and the path is squinted in a zigzag way which increases the measurement of the walk. So Mr. Barrow and I, with our followers, set off. We reached the foot of the mountain on horseback, and dismounted when we could ride no more – indeed, nothing but a human creature or an antelope could ascend such a path.

First we had to scramble up the side of a perpendicular cascade of a hundred feet, the falls of which must be very fine after the rains, and the sides of which were shaded with myrtles, and sugar trees, and geraniums.

We continued our way through a low foliage of pretty heaths and evergreens; the sun was at last beginning to beat down on our heads. It made me smile to see signs of human footsteps, in the numbers of old soles and heels of shoes which I came across here and there. I suppose relics have lain time immemorial, as leather, I believe, never decays, or not for a great while. It proved that the Dutchmen told fibs when they said that few people had tried to get up this mountain.

The heat and fatigue obliged me frequently to sit down; and as I had an umbrella, a few minutes always revived me. At about twelve o'clock, the sun became so hot that I rejoiced at the turn of the mountain, which brought us into shadow before reaching the great gully, from where we would get to the top. Redoubling our steps, we made the turn at last, and wonderful was the chill which came over us; we looked at our thermometers, and in a second they had fallen under the shadow by fifteen degrees. We had now come to a fine spring of water, dropping from the top of the rock, or near it, right over our heads. We drank some of this with port wine, and I saved a bottle of it for you, *cher ami* . . . Opposite there was a cave cut into a rock, sometimes inhabited by runaways, of which there were still traces.

Once more we set off, and in three hours reached the tip-top of the great rock, looking down on Cape Town with conscious superiority, and smiling at the formal meanness of its appearance, which would have led us to think it was built by children out of half a dozen packs of cards. I was glad to have a bird's-eye view of the country – the bays, and the near and the far mountains.

On the top of the mountain there was nothing of the luxuriancy of verdure and foliage described by other climbers; there were roots and flowers, and a beautiful heath on the edge of the rocks. The soil was cold and swampy, and mossy, covered with half an inch of water and sprinkled with little white pebbles . . . dozens of which I gathered to make Table Mountain earrings for my fair European friends.

From *Letters, Vol 1, 1797–1801*

MATSUO BASHO

– The Vast Journey Ahead –

I t was the twenty seventh day of the third month
(16 May). There was a wan, thinning moon, and
in the first pale light of dawn, the summit of Mount
Fuji could be dimly seen. I wondered if I should ever
see the cherry trees of Ueno and Yanaka again. sMy
closest friends, who had gathered together the night
before, got on the boat to see me off. We disembarked at Senju, and my heart was overwhelmed by
the prospect of the vast journey ahead. Ephemeral
though I knew the world to be, when I stood at the
crossroads of parting, I wept goodbye.

> the spring is passing –
> the birds all mourn and fishes'
> eyes are wet with tears.

I wrote this verse to begin my travel diary, and
then we started off, though it was hard to proceed.
Behind, my friends were standing in a row, as if to
watch till we were lost to sight . . .

We barely managed to reach the post town of
Sōka by nightfall. My greatest burden was the pack
I carried on my thin, bony shoulders. I had planned
to set out travelling light, but had ended up taking

a paper coat to keep out the cold at night, a cotton dressing gown, rainwear, and ink and brushes, as well as various farewell presents that I could not refuse and that had to be accepted as burdens on the way.

From *The Narrow Road to the Deep North*, 1694, translated by Tim Chilcott, 2004

– Flocks of Parrots Conceal the Sun –

I had arrived, off this islet, Bird Rock, Bahamas, – and anchored. After some time I walked on shore, and found but one house, where there was no one; and I supposed they had fled from fear, for all their property was left in the house. I would not allow a thing to be touched, and set out with the captains and people to explore the island. If the other islands already seen were beautiful and fertile, this one was more so. Here are lagoons, with wonderful vegetation on their banks. The island is all green, and the herbage like April in Andalusia. The songs of the birds were so pleasant that it seemed a man would never want to leave the place. Flocks of parrots concealed the sun; and birds were so numerous, and of so many different kinds, it was wonderful. There were trees of a thousand sorts, and all have several fruits; and I feel I am the most unhappy man in the world not to know them, for I am assured they are valuable. I will bring home specimens, and also of the land. Then, walking around one of the lakes, I saw a serpent – which we killed – and I will bring home the skin for your Highnesses. It slid into the lagoon, and we followed, as the water was not very deep, and we killed it with lances. It is 7 palmos long, and I believe there are many like it in these lagoons. Here I also came upon some *aloes,* and I have determined to take ten quintals on board tomorrow, for they tell me they are worth a good deal.

Also, while wandering for good water, we came to a village about half a league from our anchorage. The people, as soon as they heard us, fled and left their houses, hiding their property in the woods. Again, I would not allow a thing to be touched, even to the value of a pin. Presently some men among them approached us, and one came quite close. I gave him some bells and glass beads, which made him very happy. That our friendship might be further increased, I resolved to ask something of him too: I asked him to get us some water.

After we had followed our steps back to the ship, the natives appeared on the beach with calabashes full of water, and delighted in giving them to us. I ordered another string of glass beads to be offered, and they said they would return again tomorrow.

From *The Journal of Christopher Columbus, During His First Voyage, 1492–3*, translated by Clements Robert Markham, 1893

IDA LAURA PFEIFFER

– Arrival in Rio –

W e would eventually come to the Praya dos Mineiros, a disgusting and dirty sort of square. Then we proceeded directly into the principal street of Rua Direita, whose only beauty consists of its breadth for walking along. It contains several public buildings, such as the Post-office, the Customhouse, the Exchange, the Guardhouse, all of which are insignificant in appearance. Anyone would pass them by unnoticed, if it were not for the number of local people loitering there.

It was not until I had been here several days that I became more used to the appearance of the people around me. I discovered many pretty figures among the young women; and handsome and expressive countenances among the dark-complexioned Brazilian and Portuguese women. The men though, regarding beauty, seem to be far less favoured.

The bustle of people in the streets is less than I had been led to expect, and not to be compared to that of Naples or Messina. The greatest amount of noise is made by the men and women who carry burdens, and especially by those who carry sacks of coffee beans en route to the different vessels. They strike up a monotonous sort of song, to the tune of which they keep going, step-by-step, which sounds very disagreeable. However, it possesses one advantage – it does warn the newly arrived in the area and affords them time to get out of the way.

From *A Woman's Journey Round The World, 1850,*
translated by H. W. Dulken, 1861

– Laughter and Chaff –

T o carry out the work, I had chosen Wisting, Hassel, and Bjaaland. And having concluded our observations, we put the kettle on to give ourselves a drop of chocolate – for the pleasure of standing *out there* in light attire had not exactly put warmth into our bodies. As we were swallowing the scalding drink, Bjaaland observed: 'I'd like to tackle this encircling straight away. We will have lots of time to sleep when we get back.' Hassel and Wisting were of the same opinion, and it was agreed they should depart immediately. Here was another example of the spirit that prevailed in our little community. We turned this meal into a breakfast – that is to say, each ate what he wanted of his bread ration, then began to ready for the work. First, three small bags of light windproof stuff were made, and in each of these was placed a paper, giving the position of our camp. In addition, each carried a large square flag of the same dark brown material, which could be seen at a distance. As flagpoles, we elected to use our spare runners, which were both long – twelve feet long – and very strong.

Thus equipped, and with thirty biscuits as an extra ration, the three men started off in the directions laid down. Their journeys were by no means free from danger, and it does honour to those who went for not raising the smallest objection, but for marching with the greatest keenness. Let us consider the risks they ran . . . our tent on the white boundless plain, without marks of any kind, may be compared to a needle in a haystack. From this the three men were to start out for a distance of twelve and a half miles. Compasses might have been good to take on such a walk, but our sledge compasses were too heavy for carrying, therefore they had to go without. They had the rising sun to go by, but who could say how long it would last? The weather when leaving was fine enough, but it was impossible to say that a change wouldn't take place. If the sun were to get hidden, their own tracks might help them; but trusting to tracks in these regions is a dangerous thing. Before you know where you are the whole plain may be one mass of driving snow, obliterating all footprints as soon as they are made. With the rapid changes of weather here, such a thing was possible.

The three risked their lives when they left the tent at 2.30 a.m.; and doubtless knew it well. But if anyone thinks that Wisting, Hassel, and Bjaaland took a solemn farewell from those of us who stayed behind – well, no. They vanished in their different directions amid much laughter and chaff together!

From *The South Pole: An Account of the Norwegian Antarctic Expedition in the 'Fram',* Vol II, 1912, translated by A. G. Chater, 1912

E. J. BANFIELD

– A Road is Born on Dunk Island –

I t has no beginning. And it ends . . . who shall say where?

Every high tide smooths away the footprints of those who use it now, just as it did the tramplings of the hosts of the past. In those free and unregulated days, figures sprawled and scampered on the hard, glistening beach; young men and girls sported there; men lazed and fought on its convenient spaces; women wandered for the serious business of food-getting. To this day, most journeying is regulated by the tide. High water drives the wayfarer to the loose, impeding sand, over which the great convolvulus sends its tireless tentacles, to be thrown back twisted and burnt by salt surges.

The ebb discovers a broad space. The bare-footed may walk for miles and be trackless, so tough and elastic is the moist sand. It was not laid with the foundation of the earth, and not compacted by heat and stress. It is still in the making – sand and coral, shell-grit and chemicals from the reef are among its component parts. One other element invokes thanksgiving – the flaked mica, with its hues of silver and gold, giving to the tide-swept track a pliancy which resists the stamp of passing generations.

Midway between high and low water is an area sensible to the airiest tread, being fitted for such by a mechanical operation. Millions of the smallest crabs possess this space, working out their destiny digging circular shafts. They have the quality of compacting the almost fluid spoil and carrying it to the surface in pellets. These are scattered about, not without design, and in such profusion that the feet of a wayfarer will press them flat. The track becomes visible as far as the eye can reach. Then the incoming waves dissolve the pellets, and efface the record of the passing of man.

As the tides ebb, so the crabs begin their work again, preparing for the next approaching walker. There is something almost great in the tireless activities of these nervous creatures, for not only do they carry compacted sand from their burrows, but spend time forming similar globes from material gathered at the surface. Digging the surface in patterns and in moulding pellets, the plaything of a moment, – so are the lives of the shy crustaceans spent.

But let's push on. There is far to go. Leaving the shore, one branch of the track crosses the high-water fold, follows the bend of a mangrove creek, through which it makes a muddy ford, and is firmly impressed across forest country where every tree is orchid-encumbered, and where the eager soil produces its own varieties. The track wriggles up and along a ridge, with glaucous grass trees standing like spears on each side, and where wattle and tough she-oaks grow leanly out of hard soil, spread with buckshot gravel, rust-coloured.

Soon the track descends into a low valley and runs through a belt of fan-palms and jungle, bordering an ever-flowering stream the banks of which are knee-deep in loam. Huge tea-trees stand in the water, their fibrous roots are matted like peat. Out of the moist coolness, the track then ascends to a pleasant forest, and drops almost imperceptibly to tea-tree flats intersected by Pandanus creeks, which bulge here and there into sedge-margined lagoons.

In this 'devil-devil' country, the track is barely the width of a human foot, and wanders like the trail of a lazy snake. Sometimes it is barely discernible, and again in soft places it broadens and deepens, for the traveller with boots has taken the place of the original soft-footed one, and horses and cattle are fond of the short-cuts which their owners design.

Here a distinct fork is made towards a river, across which, Nature, the first of the bridge-builders, afforded an easy passage by throwing down a huge tree. It spans bank to bank, and the wood is worn to slippery smoothness by the passing of shoeless feet. The track leads through forest and jungle and mangrove belts to another river, and then away south.

The western branch keeps to forest and jungle, following the ridges. In the wet season the grass lands are flooded, and the track is like a silvery grey ribbon on a carpet of green. With careless indecision it trends further west; an angle here and a curve there, dipping and twisting, crossing gullies and creeping up slopes. The men whose feet made it in ancient days knew all the landmarks around, for mostly it keeps to sound ground.

Imagination may follow the folk of bygone days as they swung past a fallen tree, where youths wandered a few yards to throw spears at white-ants' nests on bloodwood-trees, and where they turned aside for a drink at the palm creek. Possibly the track deviated to follow the run of a scrub turkey, or because the boys knew of a scrub hen's mound, where rich pink eggs were raked out by the girls. It was girl's work to overhaul the mounds – the boys did not like digging with their hands. There was a turn leading to a huge tree where bees hived; and another turn straggled up the creek to a pool where eels secreted themselves in the moist and decaying leaves.

It is six miles from the beach, where those crabs lay the way with their pellets. Now the track skirts around swamps, follows the bends of a river, passes through forest and jungle – and is lost in vagueness and indecision.

When it was ordained that roads should be built in the interests of settlers, it was natural that the original track be followed. On the plan, a formal road runs an erratic course, for in many places it is faithful to the old footpad. Some of the zigzags of the past, some of its elbows and angles, its lines and curves, have been copied and confirmed. For the bush track is one of those fundamental things, no more obliterated by the trivialities of art than is the sand of the shore – and the illimitable crabs.

From *Tropic Days,* 1918

En Route

We walked on . . . well, of course, we were
constantly walking on.

– Nicholas Luard

MARK TWAIN

– A Dandy in Geneva –

The 'sights' of Geneva are not numerous. I made one attempt to hunt up the houses once inhabited by those two disagreeable people, Rousseau and Calvin, but had no success. I found it was easier to propose to do that than to actually do it; for the town is a bewildering place. I got lost in a tangle of narrow and crooked streets, and stayed lost for an hour or two. Finally I found a street which looked familiar, and said to myself, 'Now I am at home, I judge.' But I was wrong; this was 'Hell' street. Presently I found another place which had a familiar look, and said to myself, 'Now I am at home, sure.' It was another error. This was 'Purgatory' street. After a little longer I said, '*Now* I've got to the right place, anyway . . . no, this is "Paradise street;" and I'm further from home than I was in the beginning.' Those were queer names – Calvin was the author of them, likely. 'Hell' and 'Purgatory' fitted those two streets like a glove, but the 'Paradise' appeared to be sarcastic.

I came out on the lake front, at last, and then I knew where I was. I was walking along before the glittering jewellery shops when I saw a curious performance.

A lady passed by, and a trim dandy lounged across the walk in such an apparently carefully-timed way as to bring himself exactly in front of her when she got to him; he made no offer to step out of the way; he did not apologize; he did not even notice her. She had to stop still and let him lounge by. I wondered if he had done this piece of brutality purposely.

He strolled to a chair and seated himself at a small table; two or three other males were sitting at similar tables sipping sweetened water. I waited; presently a youth came by, and this fellow got up and served him the same trick. Still, it did not seem possible that anyone could do such a thing deliberately. To satisfy my curiosity I went around the block, and sure enough, as I approached, at a good round speed, he got up and lounged lazily across my path, fouling my course exactly at the right moment to receive all my weight. This proved that his previous performances had not been accidental, but intentional.

I saw that dandy's curious game played afterwards, in Paris, but not for amusement; not with a motive of any sort, but simply from a selfish indifference to other people's comforts and rights. One does not see it as frequently in Paris as he might expect to, for there the law says, in effect, 'it is the business of the weak to get out of the way of the strong.' We fine a cabman if he runs over a citizen; Paris fines the citizen for being run over. At least so everybody says – but I saw something which caused me to doubt it; I saw a horseman run over an old woman one day – the police arrested him and took him away. That looked as if they meant to punish him.

It will not do for me to find merit in American manners – for are they not the standing butt for the jests of critical and polished Europe? Still, I must venture to claim one little matter of superiority in our manners: a lady may traverse our streets all day, going and coming as she chooses, and she will never be molested by any man; but if a lady, unattended, walks abroad in the streets of London, even at noonday, she will be pretty likely to be accosted and insulted – and not by drunken sailors, but by men who carry the look and wear the dress of gentlemen. It is maintained that these people are not gentlemen, but are a lower sort, disguised as gentlemen.

The most degraded woman can walk American streets unmolested, and she will encounter less polish than she would in the Old World, but she will run across enough humanity to make up for it.

The music of a donkey awoke us early in the morning, and we rose up and made ready for a pretty formidable walk – to Italy! But the road was so level that we took the train.

From *A Tramp Abroad,* 1880

VERNON LEE

– The Compost of Rome –

T he Catacombs of Santa Domitilla in Via Sette Chiese – with Maria, Guido and Pascarella. The impression was of walking miles by taper-light between those close walls of brown friable stone, or that soft dusty ground, in a warm vague stifling air. The monotonous rough sides, the monotonous corners, the widenings in and out of little Galla Placidia-like crypts, with rough-hewn pillars and faded frescoes; of the irregularly cut pigeon-holes, where bits of bone moulder, and the brown earth seems half composed of bone.

That brown soft earth of the Catacombs. The stuff you would scratch off the damp walls with your nail; rotting stone and rotting bone: the very soil of Rome. Lilackish like cocoa, friable, light, which used somehow to give me the horrors as a child; the soil in which the gardener of S. Saba grows his pinks and freesias without a spade or hoe visible anywhere; the soil which seems to demand no plough; the farthest possible from that honest and stiff clay, demanding human work, of nature. The Roman soil, a *compost* as Walt Whitman would say, ready manured! The work of man in this earth (of which a pinch transported into church front or roof produces great tufts of fennel and wild mignonette), the work of man in it merely to have died! No sense of the ages in these Catacombs, or of the solemnity of death, or of the sweetness of religion; walking down black narrow passages gutted for centuries, the poor wretched human remains (save those few turned up by the modern spade), packed, sent off, made presents of, sold to all the churches and convents of Christendom; bits of bones in cotton wool, with faded labels, in glass cases, such as we see in sacristies, or enclosed in glories of enamel and gold. But all gone, gone! Those poor humble inhabitants, who were so anxious to be entire for the resurrection of the body – patrician ladies, slaves, soldiers, eunuchs, theologians – all gone piecemeal over the distant earth. The corridors swept and empty, the pigeon-holes with only a little brown cocoa-like dust.

It was raining all day, dull, dismal. Yet coming out of that place, out of that brown crumbly darkness, what was not the interest in the wet grey sky. How great the beauty, the movements of the lazy clouds. How complex and lovely the bare lane of wattled dry reeds – the exquisiteness of patches of green corn, of a few scant pink blossoms, of the shoots of elder. I remember the solemnity of the subterranean tombs at Perugia; the grisliness of the Beauchamp crypt at Warwick. But these catacombs, emptiness, desolation and that old brown lilacky, crumbly

Roman earth, in which no plough need move nor spade, – that *terriccio* . . . that pot-mould of the past.

From *The Spirit of Rome*, 1906

JULIA PARDOE

– Jog-trotting –

One little adventure did befell me on my second visit to Belém near Lisbon, which trivial in itself, struck an unpleasant impression at the time. I had made acquaintance with a Monk of the order of Mendicant Friars. He was good humoured and garrulous, and was often the human whetstone on which I sharpened my dull Portuguese. This man, accompanied by three more of the brotherhood, and attended by two boys in white surplices, bearing torches, was in the habit of perambulating the streets at night, tinkling a little handbell, and carrying a basket into which pious passersby cast such coins as they could spare for the wants of their community, and for which they received a very civil and official blessing. I made a point of obtaining one of these cheaply purchased benisons on every occasion, not from any great faith in its efficacy, but to gratify my friend, Friar António.

One evening the tinkle of the bell summoned me to the balcony, and I saw there was something unusual in the procession below; the number of persons was greater, and they were moving at a jog-trot, very inimical to the interests of charity. As they jogged nearer, I saw by the fierce light of the torches that four of the men bore some burden; and looking more attentively, I discovered its nature – it was a corpse, stretched on its back in a long wooden tray, precisely like those made use of in England by butchers. The dead man was in full costume, evidently dressed in his best, and what excited the greatest horror was the fact that the tray was too short for the body – the head, the arms, and the legs were hanging over it, and jerking up and down as the bearers jog-trotted along the roughly laid flagstones. This process of interment, I was told by an Officer, who had the curiosity to leave our house and follow the jog-trotting, was as summary as the procession to the grave – the man's 'narrow bed' was also a frightfully shallow one, the face of the corpse not being more than three inches lower than the surface of the earth; and into this misshapen grave he was flung without the least ceremony. A slight covering of soil was scattered over him, and then came the last horror of this humiliating mode of interment. The sexton jumped upon the body, and with a heavy wooden rammer literally reduced it to a jelly!

The reason given to my officer friend for this savage proceeding was that it would prevent stray dogs from tearing up the body – and this because they lacked the energy to bestow upon a fellow Christian his own coffin and a grave.

From *Traits and Traditions of Portugal*, 1833

MIRZA ABU TALEB KAHN

– Dublin Girls –

B oth sides of the street are lighted by lamps suspended in glass vases at the height of ten or twelve feet from the pavement; and the addition of numerous candles in the shop windows render it as light as day. One of the streets thus fitted up – when several chemist shops containing glass vases are filled with different coloured liquids – put me in mind of the *Iman Bareh* (Mausoleum) at Lucknow, as illuminated during the reign of the late Nabob Assuf ad Dowleh. This being the first town I had seen well-lighted at night, it impressed me with a great idea of its grandeur, and it did not suffer in any comparisons to London.

Now the crowds of people who constantly walk the streets is astonishing. They have acquired such dexterity of habit that they never run into each other. And I could not help admiring some girls who, either from the coldness of the weather or from a natural high flow of spirits, disdained to walk deliberately – no, they *bounded* through the crowd, without touching anyone else, as if they had been going down a dance.

From *Travels of Mirza Abu taleb Khan in Asia, Africa, and Europe*, 1814, translated by Charles Stewart, 1814

FRANZ HESSELL

– Berlin Empathy –

W alking slowly down bustling streets is a particular pleasure. Awash in the haste of others, it's a dip in the surf. But my dear fellow citizens of Berlin don't make it easy, no matter how nimbly you weave out of their way. For I attract wary glances whenever I try to play the flaneur among the industrious; I believe they take me for a pickpocket. The swift, firm, big city girls with their insatiably open mouths become indignant when my gaze settles on their sailing shoulders and floating cheeks. That's not to say they have anything against being looked at. But the slow motion stare of the impassive observer unnerves them. They notice that nothing lies behind my gaze.

No, there's nothing behind it. I simply like to linger at first sight; I'd like to capture and remember these glimpses of the city in which I live.

In the quieter outlying districts, incidentally, I'm no less of a spectacle. There, in the north, is a square with wooden scaffolding, the skeleton of a market, and right beside it, the widow Kohlman's general store, which also sells rags; and above the bundles of newspaper, bedsteads, and fur rugs, on the slatted veranda of her shop, there are pots of geraniums. Geraniums – vibrant red in a sluggish grey world – into which I'm compelled to gaze for a long time. The widow gives me the evil eye. But she doesn't complain – maybe she thinks I'm an inspector, something's amiss with her papers. But I mean her no harm. I'm curious about her business and her views on life.

When twilight falls, old and young women lean at the windows, propped up on pillows. I feel for them what psychologists describe with words like 'empathy'. But they won't allow me to wait alongside them. I wait alone and for nothing . . .

At times, it is my wont to go into the courtyards. In Berlin, where buildings may be several court-yards deep, life beyond the front dwellings becomes denser and more profound, making the courtyards rich in spirit, those poor courtyards with a bit of green in one corner, the carpet rods, the garbage cans, and the pumps left over from the time before running water. Ideally, I like to visit them mid-mornings, when the singers and the violinists merge, or the organ grinder man . . .

Then I stand next to the old porter woman – or rather the doorman's mother. She takes no offence at my presence, and I'm allowed to look up into the courtyard windows. The windows are all bare. Only one, on the second to top floor, has curtains. A birdcage hangs there, and when a violin cries out, from the depths of its heart, then the canary starts to warble, the only voice from the silently staring windows. It is beautiful . . .

Around here, you have to have purpose, otherwise you're not allowed. Here you don't walk, you walk *somewhere.* It's not easy for the likes of me.

From Walking in Berlin, 1929, translated by
Amanda De Marco, 2016

HERMAN MELVILLE

– Constantinople, From the Top –

Saturday December 13th

W alked out; saw cemeteries, where they dumped garbage. Sawing wood over a tomb. Forests of cemeteries. Intricacy of the streets. Started alone and after a terrible long walk, found myself back where I started. Just like getting lost in a wood. No plan to streets. Pocket-compass. Perfect labyrinth. Narrow. Close, shut in. If one could get up aloft, it would be easy to see one's way out. If you could get up into a tree. Soar out of the maze. But no. No names to the streets. No numbers. No anything. Breakfast at 10 a.m. To Seraglio. Holy ground. Crossed some extensive grounds, gardens. Fine buildings of the Saracenic style. Saw the Mosque of St Sophia. Walked in. Rascally priests demanding 'bakshesh'. Fleeced me out of ½ dollar; following me round, selling the fallen mosaics. Ascended a kind of horse-way leading up, round, round. Came out into a gallery fifty feet above the floor. Superb interior. Precious marbles and Porphyry Verd antique. Immense magnitude of the building. Names of the prophets in great letters. Roman Catholic air to the whole. Then to the Hippodrome, near which stands the six-towered mosque of Sultan Achmet; soaring up with its snowy spires into the pure blue sky, like lighthouses. Nothing finer. In the Hippodrome saw the obelisk with Roman inscription. Also a broken monument of bronze, representing three twisted serpents erect upon the tails. Meads broken off. Also a square monument of masoned blocks. Leaning over, frittered away – like an old chimney stack. Then saw the 'Burnt Column'. Black and grimy enough, hooped about with iron. Stands soaring up from among a huddle of old wooden rookeries. A more striking fire monument than that of London. Then to the Cistern of 1001 Columns. You see a rounded knoll covered with close herbage. Then a kind of broken cellar way, you go down & find yourself on a wooden, rickety platform. Two tiers of pillars one standing on t'other; lower tier half buried. Here and there a little light percolates through from breaks in the keys of the arches; where bits of green straggle down. Used to be a reservoir. Now full of boys twisting silk. Great hubbub. Flit about like imps. Whir of the spinning jennies. In going down, (as into a ship's hold) and wandering about, have to beware the innumerable skeins of silk. Terrible place to be robbed or murdered in. At whatever point you look, you see lines of pillars, like trees in an orchard arranged in the quincus style. Walked out. To the Bazaar. A wilderness of traffic. Furniture, arms, silks, confectionery, saddles, shoes – everything. Covered overhead with stone

35

arches, with side openings. Immense crowds strolling. Georgians, Armenians, Greeks, Jews. Turks are the merchants. Magnificent embroidered silks, gilt sabres, caparisons for horses. You lose yourself, are bewildered, confounded with the labyrinth, the din, the barbaric confusion of the whole. Walked to the Watch Tower, within a kind of arsenal. The Tower of vast girth and height in the Saracenic style – a column. From the top, my God, what a view! Surpasses everything. The Propontis, the Bosphorous, the Golden Horn, the domes, the minarets, the bridges, the men of war, the cypresses. Indescribable.

From *Journal of a visit to Europe and the Levant, 1856–1857*

EDITH WHARTON

– Good-by to Fez –

I t is well to bid good-by to Fez at night – and a
moonlight night for choice. Then, after dining at
the Arab inn of Fez Eldjid – where it might be incon-
venient to lodge, but where it is extremely pleasant
to eat kouskous under a grape-trellis in a tiled and
fountained patio – one may set out on foot and stray
down the lanes towards Fez Elbali.

Not long ago the gates between the different
quarters of the city used to be locked every night
at nine o'clock, and the merchant who went out to
dine in another part of the town had to lodge with
his host. Now this custom has been given up, and
one may roam untroubled through the old quarters,
grown as silent as the grave after the intense life of
the bazaars has ceased at nightfall.

Nobody is in the streets. Wandering from
ghostly passage to ghostly passage, one hears no
step but that of the watchman with staff and lantern. Presently there appears, far off, a light like
a low-flying firefly. As it comes nearer, the light is
seen to proceed from the *Mellah* lamp of open-work
brass that a servant carries ahead of two merchants
on their way home from Elbali. The merchants are
grave men: they move softly and slowly on their fat

37

slippered feet, pausing from time to time in confidential talk. At last they stop before a house wall with a low blue door barred by heavy hasps of iron. The servant lifts the lamp and knocks. There is a long delay; then, with infinite caution, the door is opened a few inches, and another lifted light shines faintly on lustrous tiled walls, and on the face of a woman servant who quickly veils herself. Evidently the master is a man of standing, and the house is well guarded. The two merchants touch each other on the right shoulder, one of them passes in, and his friend saunters off through the moonlight, his servant's lantern dancing ahead.

But here we are in an open space looking down one of the descents to El Attarine. A misty radiance washes the tall houses, the garden walls, the archways; even the moonlight does not whiten Fez, only turns its gray to tarnished silver. Overhead in a tower window a single light twinkles: women's voices rise and fall on the roofs. In a rich man's doorway servants are sleeping, huddled on the tiles. A cock crows from somebody's dunghill; a skeleton dog prowls by for garbage.

Everywhere is the loud rush or the low crooning of water, and over every wall comes the scent of jasmine and rose. Far off, from the red purgatory between the walls, sounds the savage thrum-thrum of an African orgy; here all is peace and perfume. A minaret springs up between the roof like a palm, and from its balcony the little white figure bends over and drops a blessing on all the loveliness and all the squalor.

From *In Morocco*, 1920

ANTHONY TROLLOPE

– Kiss-in-the-ring, Port Elizabeth –

I found my way to the public park and the public gardens. I cannot say they were perfect in horticultural beauty and in surroundings, but they were spacious, with ample room for improvement, well arranged as far as they were arranged, and with a promise of being superior to anything in Cape Town. The air was as sweet as any I have ever breathed. Through the gardens I went, leaving the town between me and the sea, and onto a grassy heath on which, I told myself, with perseverance I might walk on until I came to Grand Cairo. I had my stick in my hand and was prepared for any lion that I might meet. But on this occasion I met no lion. After a while I found myself descending into a valley – a pretty little green valley, out of sight of the town. And, which, as I was wending along, seemed at first to be an interruption on my way to the centre of the continent. But as I approached the verge from which I could look down into its bosom, I heard the sound of voices, and when I had reached a rock which hung over it, I saw beneath me a ring, as it might be of fairy folk, in full glee, – of folk, fairy or human, running hither and thither with extreme merriment and joy. After standing awhile and gazing

I perceived that the young people of Port Elizabeth were playing kiss-in-the-ring. Oh, how long ago was it I had played kiss-in-the-ring, and how nice I used to think it was! It was many many years since I had even seen the game. And these young people played it with an energy and an ecstasy which I had never seen equalled. I walked down, almost amongst them, but no one noticed me. I walked among them like Rip Van Winkle – I was as a ghost. They seemed not to even see me. How the girls ran, and could always escape from the lads had they wished, but were always caught out of the circle. And how awkward the lads were in kissing, and how clever were the girls in taking care that it should always come off at last. But this was merely the cynical regard of an old man.

There I left them when the sun was setting, still hard at work, and walked back sadly to my dinner at the club.

From *South Africa,* 1878

MARY GAUNT

– The Lonely Man's Walk –

It was Easter Saturday, and my new friend suggested I should spend Easter with him. I demurred, and he said it would be a charity. He had no words to express his loneliness, and as for the canoe-men, who could not stay to carry my things to Anum, let them go. He would see about my gear being taken up there. And so I stayed, glad to see how a man managed by himself in the wilderness.

The British Cotton-growing Experimental Farm at Labolabo is to all intents and purposes a failure. The farm should be a valuable possession besides being a very beautiful one. The red-roofed bungalow is set in a bay of the high, green hills, which stretches out verdure-clad arms, which threaten every moment to envelop it. The land slopes gently, and as I sat on the broad verandah, through the dense foliage of the trees I could catch glimpses of the silver Volta a mile and a half away, while beyond again the blue hills rose range after range till they were lost in the bluer distance. Four years ago, this man who was entertaining me so hospitably, had planted a mile-long avenue to lead up to his bungalow, and now the tall grape-fruit and shaddock in front of his verandah meet and are regularly cut away to keep the walkway clear. I am too ignorant to know what could be grown with profit, I can only see that the land is rich and fruitful, and should be, with the river close, a valuable possession. As it is, it is one of the loneliest places in the world . . . the loneliness grips . . . I sympathised deeply with the man living there alone. If I went to my room I could hear him tramping monotonously up and down the verandah. 'Tramp, tramp . . . tramp, tramp' – and when I went out to him, he smiled.

'I can't help doing it,' he said, 'it's the lonely man's walk. And when I can't see those two lines,' he pointed to two boards in the verandah, 'then I know I am drunk, and I go to bed.'

From *Alone in West Africa*, 1912

– Baobab Leaves for a Sore Foot –

T he sore on my foot grew worse. The month of August continued stormy; the rain poured down day and night; the sky was cloudy and the air heavy and cool. At intervals an east wind blew and was followed by a small, cold rain. The sun rarely appeared. My hut was exceedingly damp. During the rainy season, the Mandingoes scarcely ever go out of doors. They lie all day in their huts, beside a great fire, and sometimes make *coussabes* to amuse themselves. When circumstance obliges them to go out, they wear a kind of clogs with wooden soles, two and a half inches thick, which keep their feet dry. The women pursue their occupations, walking off to procure wood and water without any regard to the state of the weather. They never wear any covering on their feet whether the ground is wet or dry.

I intended to set out at the end of August; but at that time another sore much larger than the first one broke out on the same foot. I suffered considerable pain, and my foot so swelled that I could not walk. I begged the old woman to procure some baobab leaves. She boiled them, and made them into a poultice which I applied to the sore. This allayed the inflammation, and in the course of two days I found myself better. Having no rags for a dressing, I was obliged to use a piece of the cotton which formed my turban. The old woman did not approve of this: she alleged it would be better to dispense with the poultices than destroy such a beautiful piece of cloth. The baobab leaves soon reduced the swelling of my foot; but the sore continued as large as ever – twice the size of a six franc piece. I dressed it with lint which I had already used, and though washed, it was not very clean and did me no good. My host, who sympathised with my misfortune, told one of his slaves to procure a root, which I recognized as having a caustic quality. He boiled it in water until it became tolerably soft, and then bruised a piece with a stone, and made a salve of it. The first day he attended me himself: after washing the wound with water from the decoction, he spread on some of the unctuous paste produced by the root, and then, instead of a rag, he bound a leaf over the sore, that had a strong aromatic smell. On the following days, the old woman dressed my foot morning and evening and consoled me with the hope of a speedy cure. In gratitude for her attention, I made her a present of a piece of coloured cloth, which pleased her exceedingly. Her son came to thank me, and asked me who had made the flowers on the cloth. I smiled and told him it had been made by the whites. He answered, still preserving his gravity, that he thought none but God could have made anything so beautiful.

I remained a month in my hut, constantly lying on the damp ground, for I was unable to walk, though I did not suffer very great pain. The month of September seemed to promise a return of fine weather; but appearances were delusive. The rains were not incessant but we had downpours every day until October. My foot got better, and I hoped to be off at the end of the month. I looked forward to my departure with no little anxiety, and not-withstanding the kindness experienced from the old woman – my old nurse – I was impatient for the moment when I would have the pleasure of bidding her farewell.

From *Travels through Central Africa to Timbuctoo; and across the Great Desert, to Morocco, performed in the years 1824 to 1828,* Vol 1, 1830

CHARLES DARWIN

– Words Fail, Mauritius –

L earned naturalists describe the scenes of the tropics by naming a multitude of objects, and mentioning some characteristic of each. To a traveller on foot this may convey some ideas, but who else from seeing a plant in an herbarium imagines its appearance when growing in native soil? Who from seeing choice plants in a hothouse, can magnify them into the dimensions of forest trees and crowd others into an entangled jungle? Who when looking in the cabinet of the entomologist for those exotic butterflies and singular cicadas, will associate such lifeless objects with the ceaseless music of the latter and the lazy flight of the former, the sure accompaniments of the still, glowing, noonday of the tropics?

When quietly walking along the shady pathways and admiring each view, I wished to find language to express my ideas. Epithet after epithet was found too weak to convey the sensation of delight, which the mind experiences. I have said that the plants in a hothouse fail to communicate a just idea of the vegetation, yet I must recur to it. The land is one great wild, untidy, luxuriant hothouse, made by Nature for herself, but taken possession of by man, who has studded it with gay houses and formal gardens.

How great would be the desire in every admirer of nature to behold the scenery of another planet! – yet to every person in Europe, it may be said, that at the distance of a few degrees from his native soil, the glories of another world are opened to him.

In my last walk I stopped, again and again, to gaze on these beauties and tried to fix in my mind an impression which at the time I knew sooner or later must fail. The form of the orange-tree, the cocoa-nut, the palm, the mango, the tree-fern, the banana, will remain clear and separate; but the thousand beauties which unite these into one perfect scene must fade away; yet they will leave, like a tale heard in childhood, a picture full of indistinct but most beautiful figures.

From *The Voyage of the Beagle*, 1839

– Dimples –

There is no way to ascend this Hill – save one, by going up by Degrees of forty-five turnes. In our Company there were onely one Frier, foure Germanes, and I, that durst attempt to climbe the mountaine. Thursday, earely at the breach of day, we sixe made for the mountaine. After diverse turnings, traversings, and narrow foot passages having come with great difficulty to the top, we entred into an umbragious Cave, joyning to, and under the Chappell, where the Frier told us that Christ did fast for forty days and, here it was, he rebuked Sathan. The Chappel which covereth the top of this high and steepy Rocke is covered, and also beautified, with an old Altar. And betweene the outward sides hereof, and the craggy face of this mountaine, only two men can walke side to side. Here we dined and refresht ourselves with water that I carried on my backe, hither from which place we saw the most part of all the Holy Land, except the North parts of Judea, Palestine, and Phenicia, and a great way into the two Arabiaes – Petrea and Deserta – and all the length of Jordan, even from Sodome to Maronah.

At last on our Returne, and fearefull of discending, none of us goe downe first. For although the

Frier led us freely upwards, downeward first he durst not goe, – and that because at the narrow end of every turning, there was betweene the upper and the lower passage of the flat face of the Rocke, nothing but dimples and holes to receive our feete, which in discending was perillous. Now the greatest danger, at every turne, was in the downe going of the first one, who was to receive us all, one by one, and put our feet in the shallow dimples, of which if any had missed, his sliding downe would have miscarried all of us over the Rocke.

Now for the noble Germanes sake, two of whom were great Barens, Signior Strowse, and Signior Crushen, and borne Vassals to the Marquesse of Hanspauch, and I, resolved to imbrace the danger. Where downe I went, receiving every one of them, at every turne, first leading their feete by my hands, and then by inveloping them with mine armes. Well, having past halfe way downewards, we came to the most scurrile and timorous Discent of the whole passage, where with much difficulty, I set safe the foure Germanes in our narrow Roade hewen out of the craggy Hill. And then I was to receive the Frier! Whence hee comming downe from above, with his Belly and face to the Rocke, holding his hands, grumbling above, the fellow fell onwards trembling; and as I was placing his feete in the holes, distempred feare brought him downe upon me with a rushling hurle . . . Whereuppon straight I mainly closed

with my left arme his body fast to the Rocke, keep-
ing strongly my Right shoulder to the same place.
For I could not have saved my selfe, and letting him
fall, but hee would have caught mee headlong with
him, over the Rocke. And yet the Germanes cryed
still to me, *Lascia ti quel furfanto cascar alia fondo con
il Diavolo, e salva caro fratello la vita vostra, viz* – 'Let
that Villaine fall to the ground with the Divell, and
save, O deare brother, your owne life.'

But I neyther would nor durst. At last his feare,
by my incouragement having left him, I suffered
him to slide softly downe betweene my arme and the
Rocke, to the solid path. Where, by and by, hee fell
downe uppon his knees, and gave mee a thousand
Blessings, vowing for this, he would doe me a good
deede before I left Jerusalem.

At last, towards the afternoone, wee safely
arrived at the foote of the Mountaine, and having
saluted the Guardian, and all the Rest, who were
ready to take journey, the Frier told his Reverence
how I had saved his life. Whereupon the Guardian,
and the other Friers, did imbrace me kindly in their
Armes, giving me many earnest and loving thankes.

From *The Totall Discourse of the Rare Adventures and
Painefull Perigrinations of Long Nineteen Yeares,* 1614

LUCIE DUFF

– Her Hand on his Shoulder in Cairo –

I f only I could speak the language I could see any-thing on my walks. Cairo is the Arabian Nights; there is a little Frankish varnish here and there, but the government and the people are all unchanged since that most veracious of books was written. No words can describe the departure of the holy Mah-mal and the pilgrims for Mecca. I spent half the day loitering about in the Bedaween tents admiring the glorious, free people. To see a Bedaween and his wife stroll through the streets of Cairo is superb. Her hand resting on his shoulder, and scarcely deigning to cover her haughty face, as she looks down on the veiled Egyptian woman who carries the heavy bur-den and walks behind her lord and master.

From *A letter to Mr Tom Taylor,* April 1863

RICHARD BURTON

– Meccan Beat –

All pilgrims hold it to be a duty to improve their time at Mecca. Not just to do their accustomed duty and devotion in the temple, but to spend their leisure time there and, as far as strength will permit, to continue at Towoaf: ie, to walk around the Beat-Allah, which is about four and twenty paces square. At one corner of the beat there is a black stone fastened and framed with silver plate, and every time the pilgrim comes to that corner, they kiss the stone, and having gone round seven times they perform two Erkaets-nomas, or prayers. The stone, they say, was formerly white and it was called Haggar Essaed, the 'White Stone'. But by reason of the sins of the multitude, it had become black, and is now called Haggar Esswaed, the 'black stone'.

The place is so frequented by people going round it that the Towoaf – the circuit they make in going around – is seldom empty of people at any time of the day or night. Many pilgrims have waited several weeks, nay months, for the opportunity of finding it so. Many will walk around until they are quite weary, then rest, and are at it again; carefully remembering that at the end of every seventh time to perform two Erkaets. This Beat is in effect the object of their devotion. The idol which they adore. Let them never be so distance from it. East or West, North or South – they will be sure to bow towards it. Sometimes there are several hundred at Twoaf at once, especially after the fourth time of service, which is after candle-lighting. And these are both men and women. But the women walk on the outside of the men, and the men are nearest to the Beat. In so great a resort as this, it is not supposed that every individual can come to kiss the stone aforementioned. Therefore, lifting the hand towards it, smoothing down the face, and using a short expression of devotion is sufficient.

When there are few men at Towoaf, the women get an opportunity to kiss the stone, and once they have got to it, do close in as they come round and walk as quickly as they can to come to it again – and keep possession of it for a considerable time. Then the men, seeing that the women have got to the place, will be so civil to let them pass by and give them leave to take their fill. When the women are at the stone, it is esteemed a rude and abominable thing to go near them, respecting the time and place.

From *Personal Narrative of a Pilgrimage to Al-Madinah and Mecca,* 1855–6

RAJA SHEHADEH

– Chorus at A'yn Qenya –

I can still remember the very first walk I took to
this village, when we spent the night sleeping on
the rocks on which I now stood. It was the summer of 1969. I was participating in the Ramallah Boy
Scout's work camp, the only time in my life I ever
did. One evening around midnight a group of us
decided to walk down to A'yn Qenya. I don't know
why. None of us knew the way.

Israeli soldiers had come through these same
hills as conquerors two years earlier. Perhaps we
thought we would be re-conquering the territory by
overcoming our fear of the dark abyss. There certainly was something liberating about the adventure.
The night was still. There was no moon to light our
way. We were eight young and uncertain men in the
dark and for the first time I understood how it was
possible to feel comfort in numbers. The thumping
of our boots was heavy and persistent. It came as a
warning to all other creatures inhabiting these hills
to move away, stay clear of our path, if they did not
wish to be crushed. One of us, Jad, cut a branch from
an old tree and held it in front of him menacingly.
None of us would admit fear. There was no question of stopping. After scrambling in the hills for a

few hours we were exhausted. We had lost our way. We sprawled on some large slabs of rock and immediately succumbed to a deep slumber. It was not a prudent thing to do. We only woke up with the sun and the sounds of the morning: the braying of donkeys, the bleating of sheep, and the distant sounds of the women calling on their children to fetch water from the spring. Despite the pain in my neck and the back of my head from using a rock as a pillow, I still remember how I was carried away by those crystal-clear village sounds reverberating across the valley. I remember wondering whether people in the village were as fond as I was of this morning chorus. Was this why they spoke so loudly to each other? Or was the reason more practical, simply a way of communicating across the hills between houses scattered on either side, using the human voice to make up for the absence of telephones?

From *Palestinian Walks:*
Notes on a Vanishing Landscape, 2008

MICHELE ROBERTS

– St Olga –

I've never been to Kyiv before. This is my first
visit to Ukraine. Everything's different: the city
streets, the language that people speak, the clothes
they wear. Guidebook and map stuffed into my
pocket, wad of local currency, notebook and thin
silk shawl in my bag, I decide just to follow my nose.
See what happens and where I end up.

We're in high summer: sweltering heat, temper-
atures very hot. Moist air presses itself against me
like a friendly animal. You can't resist this heat: you
have to yield to it, let go into it. Sweat! Indeed the
street smells of sweat, and of petrol and perfume; of
tobacco and dust and flowers. The smell of summer,
the smell of a long day gently winding down.

Reaching the top of the hill, its brow half-
encircled by a park thick with trees, I emerge into
a long piazza running between two huge churches.
They rear up, curved and white as eggs, at either
end. The gold domes of St Michael's monastery face
the answering gold domes of St Sophia's cathedral.
I zigzag back and forth, watching groups of sauntering people: tourists, locals, a wedding party, a pho-
tographer and a bunch of models. Young women
stroll in stately groups, showing off their elaborate

hairdos and heavy makeup, short tube skirts, stiletto heels. The Ukrainian fashion student I met on the plane coming over told me that the clothes in her native city were awful. They're certainly distinctive. A version of femininity involving lots of ruching and frills. These outfits don't seem modern at all. I'm in a time warp, surely, back in the 1960s, when blank-faced girls with backcombed bouffants, thick green eyeshadow and fake eyelashes looked strangely matronly; not like girls at all.

Here comes a short, stout, middle-aged man, wearing a heavy brown suit despite the heat. He marches proudly along, clasping the outstretched hand of a very young woman. She's wearing a calf-length sleeveless frock of sugar-pink nylon, tightly gathered and full. Her hair is a puffed mass of rolled curls; her lips and fingernails shine like coral. She tittups towards me, clocks my gaze. Her escort gazes around, beaming at his audience. Look at my princess in pink! She's on display; a sparkling doll he's just bought in a shop. She gives me a mocking half-smile. Perhaps he's her father. Perhaps they're in love. Perhaps they're on their way to a party. The milling crowd surrounds them. They vanish. A carillon chimes prettily from the gold onion dome of St Michael's high above us. I turn to go.

How to leave this vast paved space and cross the road? The traffic lights aren't working. Traffic cops direct the speeding cars, man the pedestrian crossings, busily wave their batons and blow their whistles, letting us know who's in control.

That's what public architecture does: controls the people, controls the flow, determines what you'll admire, how you'll move. In 1936, a friend explained to me, the Bolshevik city bosses planned to turn this square into a vast circular space – a circus – dominated by a huge statue of Lenin. They started off by blowing up the monastery of St Michael, because it was in the way. Next, they built one curved building in approved Totalitarian Empire style. That was as far as they got, before war took over. Now, as a symbol of Ukraine's independence, the monastery has been rebuilt. On its dazzling white exterior wall, plaques record, in several languages, the Stalin-induced famine in the 1930s that caused the mass deaths of Ukrainian citizens. Kyiv is a city haunted by its terrible history. Just along the road is Babi Yar, where tens of thousands of Jewish people were slaughtered by the Nazis in September 1941. Today, in the centre of this huge square linking St Michael's and St Sophia's, an ugly sculpture commemorates not the Father of the Russian Revolution but the two male saints who introduced the Cyrillic alphabet to Ukraine, and St Olga, the tenth-century princess who introduced Christianity. When she wasn't hobnobbing with the Emperor Constantine, her godfather, she was a ruthless fighter in defence of her homeland: when she and her people were attacked, she tied brands to the tails of doves, lit them, launched them at her enemies' camps, and burned them to the ground. Any survivors were buried alive.

I leave Olga and the traffic policemen behind, turn off the square, and go down a cobbled street curving away from the crest of the hill. Here, the houses are painted apple green and salmon pink. Souvenir booths line the pavement. Too late to shop, though. Blue dusk is deepening, and the stallholders are packing up. The streets are emptying rapidly. The criminals patrol this patch at night, my Ukrainian friend said casually on the phone yesterday: but you'll be OK, they won't mug you while it's still light. I glance nervously at the shadows thickening between the boarded-up stalls. Above me rears a blue stucco church, its white columns topped with gold capitals, its dark green dome beaded with gold. Surely no-one will mug me just outside a church?

I've no time to test out this fantasy: a mass howling erupts in a nearby side street and a pack of dogs shoots out, growling and barking aggressively. I jerk in shock and panic, convinced they'll attack me, tear me to pieces, eat me for tea. One dog barking at me is bad enough; a gang of wild strays, braying and snarling, turns my insides to water. I flee, hurtle round a corner, plunge into a network of small streets. Relief. The dogs don't follow me. I stop, lean against a wall, get my breath back. What a coward I am!

I remind myself that I worked out years ago that fear of ravening hounds is projected fear of my own aggression, my own voracious hunger and rage. If I owned up to these feelings more often, I wouldn't be so frightened of dogs. OK. I swear to recognise feeling tempted to bite, snarl, scratch. I swear to become more like princess Olga and keep a bunch of burning brands in my handbag, just in case. But only one dog at a time, please.

Now I haven't a clue where I am – nor how to walk back.

From *Dusk Walks,* BBC Radio 3, 2010

– Towards the Narva Gate –

S hall we go straight towards the gate, or a round-
about route to avoid the soldiers?'

'No', I shouted, 'we go straight *through* them.
Courage! Death or Freedom!'

And the crowd shouted in return, 'Hurrah!'
And we started forward, singing in one mighty voice
the Tsar's hymn, 'God Save thy People.' But when
we came to the line, 'Save Nicholas Alexandrovitch',
some of the men belonging to the Socialist Party
were wicked enough to substitute the words, *'Save
George Appolonovitch,'* while others repeated the
words 'Death or Freedom!'

The procession moved as a compact mass. In
front of me were my two bodyguards and a young
fellow with dark eyes, from whose face a hard labour-
ing life hadn't yet wiped away the light of youthful
gaiety. On the flanks of the crowd ran the children.
Some of the women insisted on walking in the first
rows, in order, they said, to protect me with their
bodies – and force had to be used to remove them.
At the start, the police did not interfere with the
procession and they moved with us, bare-headed, in
recognition of the religious emblems.

Two local officers marched in front, preventing any hindrance to our advance, and making a few carriages coming headlong to turn aside in our favour. In this way we approached the Narva Gate; the crowd becoming more packed as we progressed, the singing more impressive, the whole scene more dramatic.

At last we reached within two hundred paces of where the troops stood. Rows of infantry barred the road, and in front a company of cavalry was drawn up, their swords shining in the cold sun. Would they dare touch us? For a moment we trembled, then started forward again.

Suddenly, the company of Cossacks galloped towards us with swords drawn. So it was to be a massacre after all! There was no time for making plans, or giving orders. A cry of alarm rose as those Cossacks came down on us. Our front ranks broke before them, opening to the right and left, and down this channel the soldiers drove their horses, striking on both sides. I saw their swords lifting and falling, our men and women and children dropping to the earth like logs of wood, moans and curses filling the air. It was impossible to think in the fever of the moment. At my order, the front rows reformed in the wake of the Cossacks, who penetrated farther and farther down the marching rows, and at last emerged at the end of the procession. Again we started forward, with resolution and rising rage in our hearts. The Cossacks turned their horses, and began to cut their way through the crowd from the rear. They passed through the whole column and galloped back towards the Narva Gate where – the infantry having opened their ranks and let them through – they formed a line. We were still advancing, but the bayonets raised in threatening rows seemed to point symbolically to our fate. Pity filled my heart, but I felt no fear.

Before we started, my dear friend, the workman K, had said to me, 'We are going to give your life as a sacrifice.' So be it!

We were now less than thirty yards from the soldiers, separated by the bridge over the Tarakanovsky Canal, which marks the border of the city. Suddenly, without warning and without a moment's delay, we heard the dry crack of rifle-shots. I was told later that a bugle had blown, but we couldn't hear it above the singing; and even if heard we wouldn't have known what it meant.

Vasiliev, with whom I was walking hand in hand, suddenly let go of my arm and sank upon the snow. One of the workmen who carried the banners also fell. One of the police officers whom I had referred to shouted out, 'What are you doing? How dare you fire upon the portrait of the Tsar?' This had no effect, and both he and the other officer were also shot down – as I found out afterwards. One was killed, the other was dangerously wounded.

I turned to the crowd and shouted to them to lie

down. I also stretched out on the ground. As we lay, another volley was fired, and another, and another, til it seemed the shooting was continuous. The crowd first kneeled, then lay flat down, hiding their heads from the rain of bullets, while the rear rows of our procession began to peel away. The smoke of the rifle-fire lay before us like a thin cloud, and I felt it in my throat. An old man named Lavrentieff, who was carrying the Tsar's portrait, had been one of the first victims. Another old man caught the portrait as it fell and carried it until he, too, was downed by the next volley. With a last gasp he said, 'I may die, but I will see the Tsar.' One of the banner carriers had his arm broken by a bullet. A little boy of ten years, carrying a church lantern, fell from yet another bullet, but held the lantern tightly and tried to rise again, before a second shot struck him. Both men who had guarded me were killed, as well as those carrying the icons and banners; and now these emblems lay scattered on the snow. The soldiers were also shooting into the courtyards of the adjoining houses, where the crowd tried to find refuge, and, as I learned later, bullets hit people inside, through the windows.

At last the firing ceased. I stood up with a few others who were uninjured and looked at the bodies lying around me. I cried to them 'Stand up!' But still they lay. I could not understand. Why did they lie there? I looked again, and saw that their arms stretched lifelessly, and I saw the scarlet stain of blood upon the snow. And I understood. And Vassilieff lay dead at my feet.

The thought flashed through my mind, 'And this is the work of our Little Father, the Tsar.' Perhaps this anger saved me – for I now realised a new chapter was opening in the book of the history of our people.

A group of workmen gathered around me. Looking back, I saw that our procession, though stretching into the distance, was broken and many of the marchers were retreating. It was in vain that I called to them, standing in the centre of these few men, trembling with indignation, amid the ruins of our movement.

From *The Story of My Life*, 1906

COLIN THUBRON

– Towards Lenin –

T he queue for Lenin's mausoleum stretches several thousands long out of parkland gardens along the Kremlin's walls, and shuffles across the grey loneliness of Red Square. In itself it resembles any ordinary Russian queue, neither more or less reverential than those for bread or beer. It is drab, dogged, muttering. All along its line it is watched by police and uniformed KGB with a lingering scrutiny. But as it turns to face the tomb, a low ziggurat in red marble, it falls silent. People remove their hats, smooth down their hair. The aura of sanctity is suddenly intense and oppressive. This is the Holy Sepulchre of atheism. The youth in front of me was told to take his hands out of his pockets. The woman behind was ordered to stop talking.

Beyond the bronze doors, flanked by two guardsmen, sombre passages enclosed us. We descended steps down walls of black and grey feldspar, which sent out faint blue lights from their stone. We were never allowed to stop moving, and can have been in the crypt for less than a minute. Light fell indirectly high above, where the decorated walls showed jagged and violently red. My eyes strained in the gloom. I was moving below the head of a glass sarcophagus framed in gilded banners, then up a half-flight of steps circling around it. Four guards stood immobile below.

Lenin lay there bigger than I had imagined, the hair fairer, sandy, and almost gone from his head. He was bathed in a brilliant white light.

From *Among the Russians*, 1983

TARAN N. KHAN

– The Look of Love –

L ove is a secret language that runs through
the streets of Kabul. In the summer of 2011,
I spent my afternoons walking the broad tree-lined
paths of Kabul University. These strolls occurred in
my imagination, through a story borne to me every
day by a young man in love.

Saleem, the lover, worked at the same TV channel where I was based. In the morning, he attended
classes on the campus, where he was an undergradu-
ate student. In the afternoon, he helped make shows
for the channel. He would appear every day after
lunch with the cups of green tea that washed down
the meal. Joining our small group crowding into
an office, he would tell us what had happened that
morning in the latest episode of his love affair. It was
our version of an afternoon soap opera.

The girl Saleem liked also studied at the university. He had spotted her in front of the faculty
building. But they had no classes together. Saleem
had no way of exchanging greetings, not even an
excuse to introduce himself. Telling her the truth
– that he really liked her – was impossible. It would
make her think he was a creep, he feared. That he
didn't understand the codes with which love could

proceed between them. He never so much as saw her alone, as she was always surrounded by her female friends. All he could do was, and what he made sure he did, was for their paths to cross on campus. He appeared in front of her and hoped to be seen; and for his presence to mean something.

The university that was the setting for these daily encounters was just a few minutes' walk from where we sat. I had walked through these relatively quiet, secluded roads numerous times. Over the years as the rest of Kabul had changed, they had managed to stay constant and welcoming, like a loved one – familiar and known. War was transforming the city yet again, impacting it more often and more directly than before. It had grown physically, climbing onto and over the slopes of its hills, and the population was estimated to be between 4 and 5 million. In 2011 there were several bloody attacks, including on a supermarket close to the heavily guarded Western embassies in Wazir Akbar Khan. The same year Osama Bin Laden was killed by US forces in Pakistan, and former Afghan president Burhanuddin Rabbani was assassinated at his home in Kabul. The US began pulling out its 'surge' troops that had arrived two years earlier. Saleem had been about ten when the Taliban had been defeated. This was his only experience of peace. This was his first love.

As Saleem spoke, I could see the paths he described – mud tracks leading off from the wider road lined with trees and neat hedges. The leaves of these trees dappling the sun on its paved surfaces. The Soviet-style buildings on the campus, some with stone seats in front. Dust and light mingling in the open spaces. The perimeter walls in the distance, and as you approached the gates, the hum of the traffic and the city outside. In Saleem's telling, this familiar terrain was overlaid with his romantic journey.

Each step was full of possibilities, each move imbued with potential heartbreak and rejection, or elation. One day, he reported, she had looked at him a little longer than she had to. One day she had lingered at a turn. One day her friends had laughed when he had appeared. Did it mean something? . . .

One afternoon, Saleem came to work thrilled. His beloved had sent him a message, through a mutual friend. She had told this friend that Saleem should style his hair in spikes more often. 'It suits him', she'd said. A code he took to mean that she's noticed him too – unlike all the other men on Kabul's streets, who she was trained to ignore, to deliberately not see, to behave as if they weren't there. By seeing Saleem she had marked him out. From that day on, Saleem's hair was impeccably spiked. His romance had entered its next phase.

From *Shadow City: A Woman Walks Kabul*, 2019

– Floral Beauties of Hindoostan –

S ome of the ladies walked a great deal. I knew one or two who used to constantly walk around the 'Course,' which is four miles long, either morning or evening. We all wore warm shawls and cloth dresses, and kept good fires in our rooms.

The station looked its best; and a walk down the road was very pleasant, with the fresh, fragrant gardens on each side, filled with sweet-scented flowers. The magnolia, with their rich fragrance, and the bright scarlet blossoms of the pomegranate contrasted with its glossy green leaves, the soft puffy golden-coloured flowers of the barbul (the 'wax flower,' as it is called, from the waxy look of its dark green leaves and white flowers), the Indian scented jessamine, various sorts of roses, and a large flower with petals like scarlet leaves, besides mignionette, larkspur, and other English types. The native flowers had either an overpowering scent, or none at all. The vegetables were all kinds of melons, potatoes, yams, cucumbers, and many others, the names of which I have forgotten. The trees were the neem, different species of acacia, mango, guava, orange, and lime, and a few bamboos (but no palms, as they do not grow so far north), and a tree which blossoms like a laburnum. These gardens were divided by green hedges. The bungalows were either whitewashed outside, or coloured according to the inmates' taste; they had no doors, as at Calcutta, but gates, and gravel walks: most of them were occupied by pet animals of some kind, deer and doves. The road was a good one, made of kunkur and planted with trees, whilst the 'Course' is edged with grass.

Having described a few of the floral beauties of Hindoostan, I must say a little for its animals. But it must be a brief mention, as I was not long enough in India to make the acquaintance of all its birds and beasts, and reptiles. I quite agree with the words of the song, 'our birds have a plumage like coloured gems' – with the exception of the vulture. I often saw this monster waddling about, gorged with food, and felt a strong inclination to shoot it.

From *A Lady's Escape from Gwalior and Life in the Fort of Agra During the Mutinies of 1857*, 1859

RABINDRANATH TAGORE

– Soul and Stomach –

Shelidah, 7th December 1894

As I walk on the moonlit sands, S usually comes up for a business talk. He came last evening; and when silence fell after our walk and talk was over, I became aware of the eternal universe there, before me in the evening light. The chatter of one person had been enough to obscure the presence of its all-pervading manifestation.

As the patter of words came to an end, the peace of the stars descended, and filled my heart to overflowing. I found my seat in a corner, with these clustered millions of shining orbs, in the great mysterious conclave of Being.

I have to walk out early in the evening, in order to let my mind absorb the tranquillity outside. Then S arrives with his jarring inquiries as to whether the milk has agreed with me, or have I finished going through the Annual Statement.

How curiously placed we are between the Eternal and the Ephemeral! Any allusion to the affairs of the stomach sounds so discordant when the mind is dwelling on things of the spirit, – and yet the soul and the stomach have been living together for so long.

The very ground on which the moonlight falls is my landed property, but the moonlight tells me that my *zamindari,* my territory, is an illusion; and my *zamindari* tells me that this moonlight is all emptiness. And as for poor me, I remain distracted between the two.

From *Glimpses of Bengal: Selected Letters*, 1921

BEATRIX BULSTRODE

– The Passing of their God –

S uddenly there is a stir, and a thrill of expecta-
tion runs through all of us. A crowd of princes
and mandarins and their sons hurries forth from the
little tents and forms up in lines on either side of
the golden pathway. Lama officials come forward
and thrust lighted joss-sticks into each of the outstretched hands. Space is left between the long rows
for three people to walk abreast.

A look of intense eagerness, even of anxiety,
spreads over the bronzed faces, for their god is but a
sick man. A harsh trumpeting presages the approach
of the incarnate deity; continuous and raucous. Two
heralds, each holding what we supposed to be a glo-
rified 'hatag' on his upturned wrists, but made of
leopard's skin stuffed in the form of an elongated
sausage, made their appearance. Following them are
the trumpeters, first one, and then the other, pro-
ducing a long unbroken wail from his copper and
brass instrument which resembles one that I bought
as a war trophy months past in Peking.

A posse of lamas in robes and the mitred head-
dress of high ceremony, looking for all the world
like a perambulating bed of nasturtiums in full
bloom, precede their pontiff, who, fat, pallid, and

ponderous, his diseased eyes protected by round black glasses, supported (held up, it seemed to us) by a priest on either side, walks labouringly along the yellow cloth. The bearers of the embroidered umbrellas are close upon his heels, and the crowd of privileged persons, priests, and laity, jostling each other for priority, follow in his train to the Temple of the Gods. Humbler lamas from remote corners of Mongolia stand about in little groups. They are there to watch the passing of their god. The feeling is tense. Fervid adoration shines from their straining eyes. Clasped hands stretch forth in expression of pro- found emotion as the procession winds its way into the temple, up to the tribute throne. There is silence, save for the sound of the heavy footsteps of the central figure as he stumps over the yellow tissue covering the boarded pathway. In an ecstasy of worship the monks prostrate themselves near the threshold of the sanctuary. They have beheld him whom they would fain see – him whom they have travelled footsore and hungry so many miles, for so many weeks, to honour. They are happy. Their faces are sublime. They have reached the haven of their desire.

Lined up along a wall not far from the great gateway to the temple, waiting with radiantly expectant countenances, and bearing gifts in their hands, are some hundreds of ragged pilgrims. Fifty guardsmen are in attendance here, ready when the time comes to marshal them into the Presence. They have been waiting since dawn, but in a state of supreme exaltation. They have drawn the lucky number amongst their fellows, and carry their offerings on trays and platters – little ornaments for the temple altars, sometimes even food, they have brought to lay at the feet of their spiritual sovereign. But their turn is not yet. Precedence has been given to the princes and rich men in fine raiment, and these, holding aloft in both hands costly tribute hidden from sight in silken coverings of daffodil yellow, make a wonderful procession as the crowd opens out for them, and they pass from a blaze of sunshine into the mellow light of the great temple interior. A low droning chant rises and falls from the throats of Urga's priests as the doors open and close on the bearers of treasure, gold, frankincense, and myrrh. They are so numerous that they can only be admitted in sections of a hundred or so at a time.

From *A Tour in Mongolia*, 1920

– At the Great Wall –

T he story of how the road got through the Wall at Shanhaikwan is interesting. It came to us in this way . . . early one summer's day, after passing through a hole in the Wall, an agriculturist hove into sight and we saluted him with: 'Lend us some light.' It is to be understood that we were not intending to light a pipe, it was simply to use an ordinary salutation as if to ask for advice. The tawny rustic stopped, gave a polite grunt after the manner of his clan, and illuminated his fine face with a liberal and benevolent smile.

'How came the hole in the Great Barrier where the iron cart passes through?' we inquired.

He gave a ready reply: 'The iron road did not make the opening; it was there long ago.'

He then related the following love story, which is the version of the people.

Many, many years ago there was a prince who was employed by the emperor in the construction of the Great Wall. For some reason or other this prince had incurred the bitter enmity of the sovereign. One day the prince mysteriously disappeared as many others did in those unhalcyon days. The story goes on to relate that this prince had married a beautiful woman who loved him tenderly and devotedly. Hearing no news of him, she undertook the long journey to the Wall in hope of discovering some clue to her lost loved one. After wandering through many perils and hardships, she arrived at her destination to learn that her husband had perished and that his body was entombed somewhere in the half-completed structure. Stricken with grief she stood weeping on the Wall, and had given up hope of even discovering her husband's remains and of bringing them back to the family burying ground, where the magic influences would waft prosperity to the family. Just then a beautiful fairy, lithe and slender, descended lightly before her and inquired of the widow the cause of her tears. 'Oh, help me to find my darling husband,' replied the half-frightened but expectant girl. 'I am so miserable and unhappy, take pity on me, please.'

'Do as I bid you,' replied the sprite. 'Cut your hand for blood that will flow from the heart, and follow the crimson drops as you walk along.'

Eagerly seizing a sharp stone, the delicate girl gashed her pretty hand, and as the blood fell, her footsteps continued until they brought her to the object of her desire, lying in an opening that had been miraculously made in the Wall. Through all the ages since, the Wall in this spot has never been repaired; and when rude, remorseless commercialism laid unholy hands on the Barrier of China to push through the parallel bars of steel, it was at this elfin path where the beautiful roaming girl found her dead lover, that the Wall was crossed and the road was made.

When the story was finished we politely said to the localite: 'We have delayed your chariot.'

He was walking.

From *The Great Wall of China*, 1909

ISABELLA BIRD

– Through Old Japan –

T he first thing that impressed me on arrival was that there were no loafers, and that all the small, kindly-looking, bandy-legged beings in the streets had some affairs of their own to mind, and to move on to.

Men sometimes walk with their children tucked into the fronts of their dresses, and I have seen as many as seven books and a map taken out of the same capacious reservoir. Many of the younger men now wear hakama, or full petticoat trousers (formerly only worn by the Samurai), drawn over the kimono with the haori outside. Foot mittens of white cloth, with a separate place for the great toe, are worn, and make the naturally small feet look big and awkward. Probably the inconvenience of the national costume for working men partly accounts for the practice of getting rid of it. It is such a hindrance even in walking, that most pedestrians have 'their loins girded up' by taking the middle of the hem at the bottom of the kimono and tucking it under the girdle. In the case of many, this shows tight-fitting, elastic, white cotton pantaloons, reaching to the ankles.

It is aristocratic for women to walk with an infirm gait, turning the feet inwards. The footgear out of doors consists of very high clogs made of the light wood of the Paulownia Imperialism, kept on the foot by a leather thong which passes between the great toe and the others. These encumbrances increase the natural awkwardness of the Japanese gait, as the foot cannot be raised in walking. The women never walk with the men, but in groups by themselves, with their children, and often carried their babies 'pick-a-back.' The men also walk with and carry children, but there were no family groups. And there were hundreds of children – dressed exactly like their parents.

I never saw people take so much delight in their offspring, holding their hands in walking, watching and entering into their games, supplying them constantly with new toys. Holding their hands on the way to picnics and festivals, never being content to be without them, and also treating other people's children with a measure of affection and attention.

Silk is everywhere. Silk occupies the best rooms of all the houses; silk is the topic of everybody's talk; the region seems to live by silk. One has to walk warily in many villages lest one will crush the cocoons underfoot, which are exposed upon mats, and look so temptingly like almond comfits.

Some of the superstitions are amusing. People always leave their clogs in the doma on entering a house, and it is believed that if you burn a moxa on the backs of those clogs of a tedious visitor, it will rid you of him. To break the thong of a clog in front, while walking, is a sign of evil to the wearer's enemies; and if at the back, to himself. In addition, few people will put on new clothes or clogs after 5 p.m. for fear of bringing bad luck . . . And if a fisherman meets a priest walking on the road, he will not catch any fish that day.

Ashi – legs
Fito – feet
Geta – clogs
Aruka – walk

A broad paved avenue, only open to foot-passengers, leads from the street to the grand entrance, a colossal two-storied double-roofed *mon* or gate, painted a rich dull red. On either side of this avenue are lines of booths, which make a brilliant and lavish display of their contents, toy shops, shops for smoking apparatus, and shops for the sale of ornamental hair pins predominating. Nearer the gate are booths for the sale of rosaries for prayer, sleeve and bosom idols of brass and wood in small shrines, amulet bags, representations of the jolly looking Daikoku, the god of wealth, the most popular of the household gods of Japan, shrines, memorial tablets, cheap ex votos, sacred bells, candlesticks, and incense-burners, and all the endless and various articles connected with Buddhist devotion, public and private. Every day is a festival-day at Asakusa; the temple is dedicated to the most popular of the great divinities; it is the most popular of religious resorts; and whether he or she be Buddhist, Shintoist, or Christian, no stranger comes to the capital without strolling its crowded courts, or making a purchase at its tempting booths. Not to be an exception, I invested in bouquets of firework flowers, 50 flowers for 2 sen, or 1d. I was also tempted by small boxes at 2 sen each, containing what look like little slips of withered pith, but which, on being dropped into water, expand into trees and flowers.

Proceeding down a paved passage on the right there is an artificial river, with a bridge formed of one curved stone, from which a flight of steps leads up to a small temple with a magnificent bronze bell. At the entrance several women were praying. In the same direction are two fine bronze Buddhas, seated figures, one with clasped hands, the other holding a lotus, both with 'The light of the world' upon their brows. The grand red gateway into the actual temple courts has an extremely imposing effect, and besides it is the portal to the first great heathen temple that I have seen. Hundreds of men, women, and children passed to and fro through the gateway in incessant streams, and so they are passing through every daylight hour of every day in the year; thousands becoming tens of thousands on the great *matsuri* days, when the mikoshi or sacred car, containing symbols of the god, is exhibited, and after sacred mimes and dances have been performed, is carried in a magnificent, antique procession to the shore and back again. Under the gateway on either side are the Ni-d or two kings. Gigantic figures in flowing robes, one red and with an open mouth, representing the Yo, or male principle of Chinese philosophy; the other green, and with the mouth firmly closed, representing the In, or female principle. They are hideous creatures, with protruding eyes, and faces and figures distorted into a high degree of exaggerated and convulsive action. These figures guard the gateways of most of the larger temples. Attached to the grating in front are a number of straw sandals and clogs, hung up by people who will pray that their legs may be as muscular as those of the Ni-d themselves.

The avenue of the Reiheishi-kaido is a good road with sloping banks eight feet high, covered with grass and ferns. At the top of these are the cryptome- ria, then two grassy walks, and between these and the cultivation a screen of saplings and brushwood. A great many of the trees become two, at four feet from the ground. Many of the stems are twenty-seven feet in girth. The trees are pyramidal, and at a little distance resemble cedars. There is a deep solemnity about this glorious avenue with its broad shade and dancing lights, and rare glimpses of high mountains. Instinct alone would tell one that it leads to something which must be grand and beautiful like itself. It is broken occasionally by small villages with big bells suspended between double poles; by wayside shrines with offerings of rags and flowers; by stone effigies of Buddha and his disciples, mostly defaced or overthrown, all wearing the same expression of beatified rest and indifference to mundane affairs; and by temples of lacquered wood falling to decay, whose bells send their surpassingly sweet tones far on the evening air.

The sun had set, and the dew was falling heavily when the track dipped over the brow of a headland, becoming a waterway so steep and rough that I could not get down it on foot without the assistance of my hands, and terminating on a lonely little bay of great beauty. There was a margin of grey sand above the sea, and on this the skeleton of an enormous whale was bleaching. Two or three large 'dug-outs,' with planks laced with stout fibre on their gunwales, and some bleached driftwood, lay on the beach. In the foreground – a solitary, dilapidated grey house, bleached like all else, where three Japanese men with an old Aino servant live to look after 'Government interests.' Only one person has passed through Lebungé this year, except two officials and a policeman.

There was still a red glow on the water, and one horn of a young moon appeared above the wooded headland. But the loneliness and isolation are overpowering, and it is enough to produce madness to be shut in forever with the thunder of the everlasting surf, which compels one to raise one's
voice in order to be heard. In the wood, half a mile from the sea, there is an Aino village of thirty houses, and the appearance of a few of the local beings gliding noiselessly over the beach in the twilight add to the ghostliness of
the scene.

From *Unbeaten Tracks In Japan,* Vols 1&2, 1880

– Warblings –

A nd now', says my friend, 'though it is growing dark, I am going to the cemetery to see what has been done at the grave. Would you like to come with me?'

We make our way over the long white bridge, up the shadowy Street of the Temples, towards the ancient hakaba of Miokoji, – and the darkness grows as we walk. A thin moon hangs just above the roofs of the great temples.

Suddenly a far voice, sonorous and sweet, – a man's voice, – breaks into song under the starred night: a song full of strange charm and tones like warblings, – those Japanese tones of popular emotion which seem to have been learned from the songs of birds. Some happy workmen are walking home. So clear is the thin frosty air that each syllable quivers to us; but I cannot understand the words:

Salté yuké toya, ano ya wo saité;
Yuké ba chika yoru nushi no soba.

'What is that?' I ask my friend.

He answers: 'A love song: *"Go forward, straight forward that way, to the house that thou sees before* *thee; – and the nearer thou walks thereto, the nearer to her* thou shalt be." '*

* Or 'him'. This is a free rendering.

From *Glimpses of Unfamiliar Japan*, 1895

THOMAS JEFFERSON

– Why Walk? –

W alking is the best possible exercise. Habitu-
ate yourself to walk very far. The Europeans
value themselves on having subdued the horse to the
uses of man; but I doubt whether we have not lost
more than we have gained, by the use of this animal.
No one has occasioned so much, the degeneracy of
the human body. An Indian goes on foot nearly as
far in a day, for a long journey, as an enfeebled white
does on his horse; and he will tire the best horses.
There is no habit you will value so much as that of
walking far without fatigue. And I would advise you
to take your exercise in the afternoon: not because
it is the best time for exercise, for certainly it is not;
but because it is the best time to spare from your
studies; and habit will soon reconcile it to health,
and render it nearly as useful as if you gave to that
the more precious hours of the day. A little walk of
half an hour, in the morning, when you first rise,
is advisable also. It shakes off sleep, and produces
other good effects in the animal economy. Rise at a
fixed and an early hour, and go to bed at a fixed and
early hour also. Sitting up late at night is injurious to
the health, and not useful to the mind.

From *The Writings of Thomas Jefferson*, 1816–1826

JOHN CHARLES FREMONT

– Bombus in the Rocky Mountains –

During our morning's hike we met no sign of animal life. A stillness and a solitude forced themselves on the mind as the main features of the place. Here, on the summit, where the stillness was absolute and the solitude complete, we thought ourselves beyond the region of animated life. But while we were sitting on the rock, a solitary bee (*Bombus,* the humblebee) came winging his flight from the eastern valley, and lit on the knee of one of the men. It was a strange place – the icy rock and the highest peak of the Rocky Mountains – for this lover of warm sunshine and flowers. And we pleased ourselves with an idea that he was the first of his species to cross the mountain barrier – a solitary pioneer to foretell the advance of civilization. I believe a moment's thought would have let him continue on his way unharmed, but we carried out the law of this country, where all animated nature seems at war, and, seizing him immediately, put him at least in a fit place – in the leaves of a large book, among the flowers we had collected on our way.

The barometer stood at 18.293, the attached thermometer at 44 degrees, giving elevation of this summit as thirteen thousand five hundred and seventy-five feet above the Gulf of Mexico, which may be called the highest flight of the bee. It was certainly the highest known flight of *that* insect.

From *Report on the Exploration of the County Lying between the Missouri River and the Rocky Mountains*, 1843

SARAH WINNEMUCCA HOPKINS

– Flower Girls, Rock Girls –

At last one evening came a beautiful voice, which made every girl's heart throb with happiness. It was the chief, and all hushed to hear what he had to say:

My dear daughters, we are told that you have seen yourselves in the hills and in the valleys, in full bloom. Five days from today your festival day will come. I know every young man's heart stops beating while I am talking. I know how it was with me many years ago. I used to wish the Flower Festival would come every day. Dear young men and young women, you are saying, 'Why put it off for five days?' But you all know that is our rule. It gives you time to think, and to show your sweetheart your flower.

All the girls who have flower-names dance along together, and those who have not got flower-names go too. Our fathers and mothers and grandfathers and grandmothers make a place for us where we can dance. Each one gathers the flower she is named for, and then they are weaved into wreaths and crowns and scarfs, and dress up in them.

Some girls are named for rocks and they are called 'rock girls', and they find some pretty rocks which they carry; each one has a rock she is named for. If she cannot take one, she can take a branch of sage brush or a bunch of rye grass, which have no flower. They all go marching along and each girl in turn is singing of herself, but she is not a girl anymore – she is a flower, singing. She sings of herself and of her sweetheart, who, marching along by her side, helps her sing the song she makes.

I will repeat what we say of ourselves – 'I, Sarah Winnemucca, am a shell-flower, such as I wear on my dress. My name is Thocmetony. I am so beautiful! Who will come and march with me while I am so beautiful? Oh, come and be happy with me! I shall be beautiful while the earth lasts. Somebody will always admire me; and *who* will come and be happy with me in the Spirit Land? I shall be beautiful there forever. Yes, I shall be more beautiful than my shell flower, my Thocmetony! Then, come, oh come, and dance and be happy with me!' The young men sing with us as they dance and march beside us.

Our parents are waiting for us somewhere, to welcome us home from our marching. And then we praise the sage brush and the rye grass that have no flower, and the pretty rocks that some of us are named for; and then we present our beautiful flowers to these companions who could carry none. And so we are all happy – and that closes the beautiful day.

From *Life Among the Piutes: Their Wrongs and Claims*, 1883

FREDERICK WHYMPER

– The Stars had Nothing Else to Do –

T he snow was fresh and soft, and all our party wore snowshoes. After a little use, I became quite proficient. The secret in wearing them is to forget you have them on at all, and to walk exactly as you would anywhere else. The snowshoe then moves forward with the foot, but is not lifted much above the snow, and the lashings are so arranged that the toe remains fixed, while the rest of the foot moves up and down in the usual manner. Of course, the great object in using them is to diffuse your whole weight over a large surface, and they are usually of a good length, sometimes five and a half feet long. An average length is four and a half feet. All of them used in this part of the country are rounded and bent upward in front, and pointed behind. They are made of birch-wood and covered at either end with a fine network of gut; the lashings for the foot are strips of hide.

> *Body – S'Kotit (in Co-Yukon)*
> *Leg – Sowool*
> *Foot – Seka*
> *Coat – Taiak*
> *Trousers – Katchee*
> *Shoes – Kakatauch*

We travelled N.N.E. magnetic, and followed pretty closely to the base of the Ulukuk Mountains, which in themselves are hills of inconsiderable altitude, not usually exceeding 3,000 feet in height. They are, however, conspicuous landmarks in a country which is otherwise fairly level. These mountains run north and south for 100 miles. One of their outlying hills, called the 'Versola Sofka,' has a very graceful and rounded form.

We occasionally stopped trekking for a draught of ice-cold water. After breaking a hole in the ice of a creek, I noticed that our Indian guide filled it up with loose snow before stooping down on hands and knees to drink. This was done to filter the water, and to prevent some little red worms, said to infest it, from being swallowed. Our route again lay through a 'peronose,' or portage, and presented alternations of open spaces and light woods of spruce fir, and birch, and willow.

At 4 p.m. we reached the base of the 'Yersola Sofka' Mountain, where we found a large frozen stream. We camped hard by it and made a glorious fire and a bed of aromatic fir-brush. A screen of canvas, fixed behind our camp to the trees, and our snow-shoes stuck in the ground, sheltered us from the only enemy we feared . . . the wind.

After having arranged the camp, we divested ourselves of our damp fur socks and skin boots, and hung them to dry at a moderate distance from the fire. One of us sliced up the bacon, got out a bag of 'hard bread,' or biscuits, or set to work concocting a stew of dried deer-meat or fresh grouse. Soon our meal was over, the ever-grateful pipe smoked by one and all, and then we turned into our blankets and furs, the stars looking down calmly upon us –

'Because they had nothing else to do,

and in a few minutes we were soundly sleeping. We woke in the morning to find our breath had congealed in masses of ice on our mustaches and on other hairy appendages.

From *Travel and Adventure in the Territory of Alaska*, 1869

SARAH H. BRADFORD

– Follow the North Star –

I'm sorry, frien's, to lebe you,
Farewell! oh, farewell!
But I'll meet you in de mornin',
Farewell! oh, farewell!
'I'll meet you in de mornin',
When you reach de promised land;
On de oder side of Jordan,
For I'm boun' for de promised land.'

T he brothers started with her, but the way was
strange, the north was far away, and all was
unknown. The masters would pursue and recap-
ture them, and their fate would be worse than ever
before. And so they broke away from her, and bidding her goodbye, hastened back to the known horrors of slavery, and to the dread of that which was
worse.

Harriet was left alone. But after watching the
retreating forms of her brothers, she turned her face
towards the north, and fixed her eyes on the guiding
star. Her farewell song was remembered in the cab-
ins, where old mother Tubman sat and wept for her
lost child. No intimation had been given to her of
Harriet's intention, and her cries and lamentations

would have been known to those who heard of Harriet's intended escape. And now with only the North Star as her guide, our heroine set off on the way to liberty. 'For,' she said, 'I had reasoned dis out in my mind; there was one of two things I had a right to, liberty, or death; if I could not have one, I would have de oder, for no man should take me alive.'

She moved through unknown regions. Walking by night. Hiding by day. Always conscious of an invisible pillar of cloud by day, and fire by night, under the guidance of which she journeyed or rested. Without knowing whom to trust, or how near her pursuers might be, she felt her way, and by native cunning or by God given wisdom, managed to apply to the right people for food, and sometimes for shelter; though often Harriet's bed was only the cold ground, and her watchers were the stars of the night.

From *Harriet, the Moses of her People*, 1886

JAMES PHINNEY BAXTER

– Quedaquae –

The following is a part of the language of the countries and kingdoms of Hochelaga and Canada.

Good Day   Aigay

A man   Aguehan
A woman   Agruette.
A boy   Addegesta
A girl   Agnyaquesta

The eyes   Hegata
The thighs   Hetnegradascon
The knees   Agochinegodascon
The legs   Agouguenehonde.
The feet   Ohchidascon

Hat   Castona
Socks   Henondous
Shoes   Atha

The sky   Quenhia
The earth   Damga.
The sun   Ysnay.

The moon   Assomaha
The stars   Siguehoham
The wind   Cahena
The sea   Agongasy
A mountain   Ogacha
The road   Adde

They call a town   Canada

Whence came you?   Canada undagneny

To walk   Quedaquae

From *A Memoir of Jacques Cartier: Sieur de Limoilou,
His Voyages to the St. Lawrence of 1534*, 1906

– San Francisco to New York on a Wager –

While boiling the cocoa, our attention was attracted by the fine figure of a man who stood on an embankment about fifty feet away, gazing down at us. He was dressed in khaki, sombrero, and leggings, and seemed preternaturally tall, silhouetted on the dull red evening sky.

'Hello, comrade,' called Dan. 'Want a bite to eat?'

The man strode down the bank and approached our fire. He was tall indeed, with the slim waist and long limbs of a track athlete. His smooth, deeply-tanned skin set off his bright blue eyes and white teeth to advantage as a real Tipperary smile curved his lips. As he removed his hat, a thatch of white hair added an incongruous touch to his appearance.

Squatting on his haunches like one accustomed to that posture, he explained he had just eaten a hearty meal, but accepted a cup of cocoa to keep us company. After listening to an account of our experiences, he said he was an ex-soldier, now walking from San Francisco to New York on a wager. He had made the trip from east to west in ninety days and was bent on returning in ten weeks. So far he had made good time and felt confident of winning.

With scant regard for the property of the railroad company, he insisted on carrying a great pile of old crossties to a secluded spot and there started a bonfire. When I considered the forty-odd miles he had covered that day, I marvelled at the man. When the fire was blazing brightly, we settled ourselves on the windward side for a real talk-feast.

His most exciting adventure on this march had occurred far out in the desert when he had been accosted by three tramps, who demanded the canteen of water he carried on his shoulder. He unslung it with the intention of sharing the precious fluid, but one attempted to snatch it from his hand. As they struggled, another approached and struck him from the rear with a rock. With a sudden sidelong leap, he wrenched himself free, and swinging the canteen by the strap with all his force, let the first man have it full in the forehead. The fellow went down without a groan and with a backhand motion, the soldier brought the canteen up and around, striking the second tramp on the point of the jaw. His companions out of commission, the third man took to his heels, while our hero gathered up the first hobo, who still lay unconscious, and with the aid of the second carried him to the rail-road track and flagged a passing freight, which took the two tramps to the next town.

As evening advanced, the Irishman entertained us with descriptions of the many strange corners of the world he had visited in the service of Uncle Sam, and told wild yarns of experiences in the Philippines and in China.

After a last creepy story of a looted temple and a dead Qiinese priest – who came to life while the foreign devils were holding high carnival, and walking into their midst in his grave clothes – we stretched ourselves beside the glowing coals and slept.

The sharp cold of early morning awakened me, and heaping the ashes high with dry wood, I kindled a fire and started breakfast. Our soldier friend lay with head on knapsack, and in the deep relaxation of sleep all harsh footprints of the years disappeared and his face looked pure and boyish in the soft light of dawn. As he whimpered with cold and weariness, I could scarcely restrain myself from easing his head with a motherly touch, but contented myself with covering him with our blankets.

Breakfast concluded, we prepared to follow our diverging paths. Then, as we said goodbye, the soldier thrust his battered canteen into my hands.

'Your need is to come, but mine is ended. Keep it in remembrance of me.'

He lifted his hat and was gone.

From *The Adventures of a Woman Hobo*, 1917

– *Hay Frutas?* –

T hen comes Sunday morning, with the peculiar looseness of its sunshine. And even if you keep mum, the better-half says: *Let's go . . . somewhere.*

But, thank God, in Mexico at least one can't set off in the 'machine'. It is a question of a meagre horse and a wooden saddle, on a donkey. Or what we called, as children, 'Shanks' pony' – the shanks referring discourteously to one's own legs.

We will go out of town. Rosalino, we are going for a walk to San Felipe de las Aguas. Do you want to go, and carry the basket?

'*Cómo no, Señor?*' It is Rosalino's inevitable answer – 'How not, Señor?'

'I will lift up my eyes unto the hills, whence cometh my strength.' At least one can always do *that*, in Mexico. In a stride, the town passes away.

We decide for the farthest speck of a village in a dark spot of trees. It lies so magical, alone, tilted in the fawn-pink slope. So alone and, as it were, detached from the world in which it lies, a spot.

The morning is still early, the brilliant sun does not burn too much. The savannah valley is shadeless, spotted only with the thorny ravel of mesquite bushes. Occasional donkeys with a blue-hooded woman perched on top come tripping in silence, twinkling, a shadow. Just occasional women taking a few vegetables to market. Practically no men. It is Sunday.

Rosalino, prancing behind with the basket, plucks up his courage to speak to one of the women passing on a donkey.

'Is that San Felipe where we are going?'

'No, that is not San Felipe.'

'What, then, is it called?'

'It is called Huayapa.'

They have spoken to each other in half-audible, crushed tones, as they always do, the woman on the donkey and the woman with her on foot, swerving away from the basket-carrying Rosalino. They all swerve away from us, as if we were potential brigands. It really gets one's pecker up. The presence of the *Señora* only half reassures them. For the *Señora*, in a plain hat of bluey-green woven grass, and a dress of white cotton with black squares on it, is almost a monster of unusualness. *Prophet art thou, bird, or devil?* the women seem to say, as they look at her with keen black eyes. I think they choose to decide she is more of the last.

Ten o'clock, and the sun is getting hot. Not a spot of shade, apparently, from here to Huayapa. The blue getting thinner on the mountains, and an indiscernible vagueness, of too much light, descending on the plain.

The road suddenly dips into a little crack, where runs a creek. This again is characteristic of these parts of America. Water keeps out of sight. Even the biggest rivers, even the tiny brooks. You look across a plain on which the light sinks down, and you think: Dry! Dry! Absolutely dry! You travel along, and suddenly come to a crack in the earth, and a little stream is running in a little walled-in valley bed, where is a half-yard of green turf, and bushes. Or you may come to a river a thousand feet below, sheer below you. But not in this valley. Only the stream.

We proceed in the blazing sun up the slope. There is a white line at the foot of the trees. It looks like water running white over a weir. The supply of the town water comes this way. Perhaps this is a reservoir. A sheet of water! How lovely it would be, in this country, if there was a sheet of water with a stream running out of it! And those dense trees of Huayapa behind.

'What is that white, Rosalino? Is it water?'

'*El Blanco? Si, aqua, Señora.*'

Probably, if the Señora had said: Is it milk? he would have replied in the same way: *Si es leche, Señora!* – Yes, it's milk.

Hot, silent, walking only amidst a weight of light, out of which one hardly sees, we climb the spurs towards the dark trees. And as we draw nearer, the white slowly resolves into a broken, whitewashed wall.

'Oh!' exclaims the *Señora.* 'It isn't water! It's a wall!'

'*Si, Señora. Es panteón.*'

'It is a cemetery,' announces Rosalino.

It was nearing midday. At last we got into a shady lane, in which there were puddles of escaped irrigation-water. This ragged semi-squalor of a half-tropical lane, led to the village.

We were entering Huayapa. *La Calle de las Minas,* said an old notice. *La Calle de las Minas,* said a new, brand-new notice, as if in confirmation. First Street of the Mines. And every street had the same old and brand-new notice: 1st Street of the Magnolia: 4th Street of Enriquez Gonzalez. Very fine!

But the First Street of the Mines was just a track between the stiff living fence of organ cactus, with poinsettia trees holding up scarlet mops of flowers; and mango trees, tall and black, stonily drooping the strings of unripe fruit. The Street of the Magnolia was a rocky stream-gutter, disappearing to nowhere from nowhere, between cactus and bushes. The Street of the Vasquez was a stony stream-bed, emerging out of tall, wildly tall reeds.

Not a soul anywhere. Everything hidden, secret, silent. A sense of darkness among the silent mango trees, a sense of lurking, of unwillingness. Then actually some half-bold curs barking at us across the stile of one garden. And then actually a man crossing the proudly labelled: Fifth Street of the Independence.

If there were no churches to mark a point in these villages, there would be nowhere at all to make for. And where there is a church there will be a *plaza*. And a *plaza* is a *zócalo*, a hub. Even though the wheel does not go round, a hub is still a hub.

So we stray diffidently on, in the maze of streets which are only straight tracks between cactuses, till we see *Reforma,* and at the end of *Reforma*, the great church.

In front of the church is a rocky *plaza* leaking with grass, with water rushing into two big, oblong stone basins. The great church stands rather ragged, in a dense forlornness, like some big white human being, in rags, held captive in a world of ants.

On the bottom of the *plaza* is a shop. We want some fruit.

'*Hay frutas?* Oranges or bananas?' –

'*No, Señor.*'

'No fruits?'

'*No hay!*'

'Can I buy a cup?'

'*No hay.*'

'Can I buy a *jicara*, a gourd-shell that we might drink from?'

'*No hay.*'

No hay means . . . *there isn't any.*

'What is there, then?' A sickly grin. There are, as a matter of fact, candles, soap, dead and withered chiles, a few dried grasshoppers, dust, and stark, bare wooden pigeon-holes. Nothing, nothing, nothing. Next-door is another little hole of a shop.

Hay frutas?

No hay.

The village is exhausted in resource. But we insist on fruit. Where, *where,* can I buy oranges and bananas? I see oranges on the trees, I see banana plants.

'Up there!' The woman waves with her hand as if she were cutting the air upwards.

'That way?'

'Yes.'

We go up the Street of Independence. They have got rid of us from the *plaza.*

Another black hut with a yard, and orange-trees beyond.

'*Hay frutas?*'

'*No hay.*'

'Not an orange, nor a banana?'

'*No hay.*'

We walk on. *She* has got rid of us. We descend the black rocky steps to the stream, and up the other side, past the high reeds. There is a yard with heaps of maize in a shed, and tethered bullocks; and a girl.

'*Hay frutas?*'

'*No hay.*'

'But Yes! There are oranges – there!'

She turns and looks at the oranges on the trees at the back, and answers:

'*No hay.*'

We hear a drum and a whistle. It is down a rocky black track that calls itself The Street of Benito Juarez.

A yard with shade round. Women kneading the maize dough, *masa*, for *tortillas*. A man lounging. And a little boy beating a kettledrum sideways, and a big man playing a little reedy wooden whistle, rapidly, endlessly, disguising the tune of *La Cucuracha*.

'*Hay frutas?*'

'*No hay.*'

'Then what is happening here?'

A sheepish look, and no answer.

'Why are you playing music?'

'It is a *fiesta.*'

My God, a feast!

The lounging man comes and mutters to Rosalino, and Rosalino mutters back, four words.

Four words in the *idioma*, the Zapotec language. We retire, pushed silently away.

'What language do they speak here, Rosalino?'

'*The idioma.*'

'You understand them? It is Zapoteca, same as your language?'

'Yes, *Señor.*'

'Then why do you always speak in Spanish to them?'

'Because they don't speak the *idioma* of my village.'

We went down every straight ant-run of that blessed village. But at last we pinned a good-natured woman. 'Now tell us, *where* can we buy oranges? We see them on the trees.'

'Go,' she said, 'to Valentino Ruiz. He has oranges. Yes, he has oranges, and he sells them.' And she cut the air upwards with her hand.

From black hut to black hut went we, till at last we got to the house of Valentino Ruiz. And it was the yard with the *fiesta*. The lounging man was peeping out of the gateless gateway, as we came.

'It is the same place!' cried Rosalino.

But we don't belong to the ruling race for nothing. Into the yard we march.

'Is this the house of Valentino Ruiz?'

Hay naranjas?

'Are there oranges?'

We had wandered so long, and asked so often, that the *masa* was made into *tortillas*, the *tortillas* were baked, and a group of people were sitting in a ring on the ground, eating them. It was the *fiesta*.

At my question up jumped a youngish man, and a woman, as if they had been sitting on a scorpion each.

'Oh, *Señor*,' says the woman, 'there are few oranges, and they are not ripe, as the *Señor* would want them. But pass this way.'

We pass up to the garden, past the pink roses, to a little orange-tree, with a few yellowish-green oranges.

'You see; they are not ripe as you will want them,' says the youngish man.

'They will do.' Tropical oranges are always green. These, we found later, were almost insipidly sweet.

Even then, I could only get three of the big, thick-skinned, greenish oranges. But I spy sweet limes, and insist on having five or six of these.

He charges me three cents apiece for the oranges: the market price is two for five cents: and one cent each for the *limas*.

'In my village,' mutters Rosalino when we get away, 'oranges are five for one cent.'

Never mind! It is one o'clock. Let us get out of the village, where the water will be safe, and eat lunch.

In the *plaza*, the men are dispersing, one gang coming down the hill. They watch us as if we were a coyote, a *zopilote*, and a white she-bear walking together in the street.

'*Adios!*'

'*Adios!*' comes the low roll of reply, like a roll of cannon shot.

The water rushes downhill in a stone gutter beside the road. We climb up the hill, up the Street of the Camomile, alongside the rushing water. At one point it crosses the road un-channelled, and we wade through it. It is the village drinking supply.

At the juncture of the roads, where the water crosses, another silent white gang of men.

Again: *Adios!* and again the deep, musical volley of *Adios!*

Up, up wearily. We must get above the village to drink the water without developing typhoid.

At last, the last house, the naked hills. We follow the water across a dry maize-field, then up along a bank. Below is a quite deep gully. Across is an orchard, and some women with baskets of fruit.

'*Hay frutas?*' calls Rosalino, in a half-voice. He is getting bold.

'*Hay,*' says an old woman, in the curious half-voice. 'But not ripe.'

Shall we go down into the gully into the shade? No, someone is bathing among the reeds below, and the aqueduct water rushes along in the gutter here above. On, on, till we spy a wild guava tree over the channel of water. At last we can sit down and eat and drink, on a bank of dry grass, under the wild guava tree.

I scoop out a big half-orange, the thick rind of which makes a cup.

'Look, Rosalino! The cup!'

'*La taza!*' he cries, with a bark of laughter and delight.

And one drinks the soft, rather lifeless, warmish Mexican water. But it is pure.

Over the brink of the water-channel is the gully, and a noise - chock, chock! I go to look. It is a woman, naked to the hips, standing washing her other garments upon a stone. In the water a few yards up-stream two men are sitting naked, also washing their clothes. Just above them is a sort of bridge, where the water divides, the channel-water taken from the little river, and led along the top of the bank. We sit under the wild guava tree in silence, and eat.

Then the old woman of the fruit comes marching down the aqueduct with black bare feet, holding three or four *chirimoyas* to her bosom. Chirimoyas are green custard-apples.

She lectures us, in slow, heavy Spanish: 'This water, here, is for drinking. The other, below, is for washing. This, you drink, and you don't wash in it. The other, you wash in, and you don't drink it.'

'Very good. We understand.'

Then she gave us the *chirimoyas*. I asked her to change the *peso*: I had no change.

'No, *Señor*,' she said. 'No, *Señor*. You don't pay me. I bring you these, and may you eat well. But the *chirimoyas* are not ripe: in two or three days they will be ripe. Now, they are not. You can't eat them yet. But I make a gift of them to you, and may you eat well. Farewell. Remain with God.' She marches impatiently off along the aqueduct.

Rosalino waited to catch my eye. Then he opened his mouth and showed his pink tongue and swelled out his throat like a cobra, in a silent laugh after the old woman.

'But,' he said in a low tone, 'the *chirimoyas* are not good ones.'

He was right. When we came to eat them, three days later, the custard-apples had worms in them, and hardly any white meat.

'The old woman of Huayapa,' said Rosalino, reminiscent.

We lay still for a time, looking at the tiny guavas and the soft, high blue sky overhead, where the hawks and the ragged-winged *zopilotes* sway and diminish. A long, hot walk home. But *mañana es otro dia*. Tomorrow is another day. And even the next five minutes are far enough away, in Mexico, on a Sunday afternoon.

From *Mornings in Mexico: Walk to Huayapa*, 1927

RACHEL CARSON

– Through a Ghost Forest –

One of my favourite approaches to a rocky sea-coast is by a rough path through an evergreen forest that has its own particular enchantment. It is usually an early morning tide that takes me along that forest path, so that the light is still pale and fog drifts in from the sea beyond. It is almost a ghost forest, for among the living spruce and balsam are many dead trees – some still erect, some sagging earthward, some lying on the floor of the forest. All the trees, the living and the dead, are clothed with silver and green crusts of lichens. Tufts of the bearded lichen or old man's beard hang from the branches like bits of sea mist tangled there. Green woodland mosses and a yielding carpet of reindeer moss cover the ground. In the quiet of that place even the voice of the surf is reduced to a whispered echo and the sounds of the forest are but the ghost of sound – the faint sighing of evergreen needles in the air; the creaks and heavier groans of half-fallen trees resting against their neighbours and rubbing bark against bark; the light rattling fall of a dead branch broken under the feet of a squirrel and sent bouncing and ricocheting earthward.

But finally the path emerges from the dimness

of the deeper forest and comes to a place where the sound of the surf rises above the forest sounds – the hollow boom of the sea, rhythmic and insistent, striking the rocks, falling away, rising again.

Up and down the coast the line of the forest is drawn sharp and clean on the edge of a seascape of surf and sky and rocks. The softness of the fog blurs the contours of the rocks; gray water and gray mists merge offshore in a dim and vaporous world that might be a world of creation . . . stirring with new life.

From *The Edge of the Sea*, 1955

– Forest Walkers in South America –

(i)

I n the morning, after a refreshing shower-bath under the mill-feeder, we shouldered our insect-nets and our pouches and, accompanied by Mr. Leavens, went on foot into the forest. On our way we saw the long-toed jacanas on the riverside, Bemtevi* flycatchers on the branches of every bare tree, and toucans flying with outstretched bills to the morning repast. Their peculiar creaking note was often heard, with now and then the loud tapping of the great woodpeckers, and the extraordinary sounds uttered by the howling monkeys – all telling us plainly that we were walking in the vast forests of tropical America.

*Bemtevi is 'I saw you well': the bird's note resembles this word.

Alfred Russel Wallace, from *A Narrative of Travels on the Amazon and Rio Negro*, 1889

I t is near sunset and, hark!, as I skirt the woods, I hear in the low scrub before me the crested tinamous (Calodromas elegans) – the wild fowl of this region, and in size like the English pheasant – just beginning their evening call. It is a long, sweetly modulated note, somewhat flute-like, and sounding clear and far in the quiet evening air. The covey is a large one, I conjecture, for many voices are joined in the concert. I mark the spot and walk on; but at my approach, however quiet and masked with bushes it may be, one by one the shy vocalists drop their parts. The last to cease repeats his note half a dozen times, then the contagion reaches him and he too becomes silent. I whistle and he answers; for a few minutes we keep up the duet, then, aware of the deception, he is silent again. I resume my walk and pass and repass fifty times through the scattered scrub, knowing all the time that I am walking amongst the birds, as they sit turning their furtive eyes to watch my movements, but concealed from me by that wonderful resemblance in their plumage to the sear grass and foliage around them, and by the instinct which bids them to sit still in their places. I find many evidences of their presence – prettily mottled feathers dropped when preening their wings, also twenty neat circular hollows scooped in the sand in which they dusted themselves. There are also little chains of footprints running from one hollow to the other; for these pits serve the same birds every day. I leave the favored haunt, yet hardly a hundred yards away the birds resume their call in the precise spot I have just quitted; first one and then two are heard, then twenty voices join in the pleasing concert. Already fear, an emotion strong but transitory in all wild creatures, has passed from them, and they are free and happy as if my wandering shadow had never fallen across them.

Twilight comes and brings an end to these useless researches; useless, I say, and take delight in saying it; for if there is anything one feels inclined to abhor in this placid land, it is the doctrine that our investigations into nature are for any benefit, present or future, to the human race.

W. H. Hudson, from *Idle Days in Patagonia*, 1917

(iii)

L eave behind you your high-seasoned dishes, your wines and your delicacies: carry nothing but what is necessary for your own comfort and the object in view, and depend upon the skill of an Indian, or your own, for fish and game. A hat, a shirt, a light pair of trousers will be all the raiment you require. Custom will soon teach you to tread lightly and barefoot on the little inequalities of the ground, and show you how to pass on unwounded amid the mantling briers. Snakes, in these forests are certainly an annoyance, though perhaps more in imagination than reality, for you must recollect that the serpent is never the first to offend; his poisonous fang was not given to him for conquest – he inflicts a wound only to defend existence. Provided you walk cautiously and do not touch him, you may pass in safety close by him. As he is often coiled up on the ground, or amongst the branches of the trees above you, a degree of circumspection is necessary lest you unwarily disturb him.

And tigers are few here, and apt to fly before the face of man, to require a moment of your attention.

Charles Waterton, from *Waterton's Wanderings in South America*, 1891

(iv)

I kept my eyes constantly turned towards the river. But picking up some spangles of mica gathered together in the sand, I discovered recent footsteps, which were distinguishable by their form and size. The animal had gone towards the forest, and turning my eyes on that side, I found myself within eighty paces of it – a jaguar, lying under the thick foliage of a ceiba. No tiger had ever appeared to me so large.

I was alarmed, yet sufficiently master of myself

to follow the advice which the Indians had given on how to act in such cases. I continued walking on without running, avoided moving my arms; and I thought I observed the jaguar's attention was fixed on a herd of capybaras crossing the river. I began to retrace my steps, making a large circuit toward the edge of the water. As the distance increased, I thought I might accelerate my walking pace. How often I was tempted to look back to assure myself I was not being pursued! Happily I yielded tardily to this desire. The jaguar had remained motionless. Those enormous cats with their spotted robes are well fed in countries of capybaras, pecaries, and deer, and rarely attack men. I arrived back at the boat out of breath, and related my adventure to the Indians. They appeared little interested by my story; yet, after having loaded our guns, they walked with us back to the ceiba under which the jaguar had lain. He was no longer there, and it would have been imprudent to have followed him into the forest, where we would have dispersed, or advanced in single file, amidst the densities of intertwining lianas.

Alexander Von Humboldt, from *Personal Narrative of Travels to the Equinoctial Regions of America, During the Year 1799–1804*, translated by Thomasina Ross, 1852

T alimeoat was a most likeable man. I was much in his company. One still evening in autumn, just before business was to take me to Buenos Aires, I went walking with him near Lake Kami. We were just above upper tree level, and before descending into the valley, rested on a grassy slope. The air was crisp, for already the days were getting short and, with weather so calm and clear, there was bound to be a hard frost before sunrise. A few gilt-edged, feathery clouds broke the monotony of the pale green sky, and the beech forest that clothed the lake's banks to the water's edge hadn't lost its brilliant autumn colours. The evening light gave the remote ranges a purple tint impossible to describe or to paint.

Across leagues of wooded hills up the forty-mile length of Lake Kami, Talimeoat and I gazed long towards a glorious sunset. I knew he was searching the distance for any sign of smoke from the camp-fires of friends or foes. After a while his vigilance relaxed and, lying near me, he seemed to become oblivious to my presence. Feeling the chill of evening, I was on the point of suggesting we walk on, when he heaved a sigh and said to himself, as softly as an Ona could say anything:

'Yak haruin.' (*'My country'*)

That sigh, followed by those gentle words, so

unusual for one of his kind – was it caused by a vision of the not so distant future, when the Indian hunter would roam his quiet woods no more; when the light wraith from his camp fire would give place to smoke from the saw-mills; when throbbing engines and hooting sirens would shatter the age-old silence? If these were his thoughts, I shared his emotions to the full. I was powerless to stop the encroachment of civilization, but I was determined to do my utmost to soften the blow of it. I was going to Buenos Aires, but I would come back, not to Ushuaia or Harberton or Cambaceres, but to Najminshk in the heart of the Ona country, where I could help the hereditary lords of the land, the people whom I was proud to call my friends.

Lucas Bridges, from *Uttermost Part of The Earth,* 1948

ERNEST SHACKLETON

– Silver Pathway, South Georgia –

T he sun rose in the sky with every appearance of a fine day, and we grew warmer as we toiled through soft snow. Ahead of us lay the ridges and spurs of a range of mountains, the transverse range we had noticed from the bay. We were travelling over a gently rising plateau, and at the end of an hour we found ourselves growing uncomfortably hot! After passing an area of crevasses we paused for our first meal. We dug a hole in the snow three feet deep with the adze, and put the Primus into it. There was no wind, but a gust might come suddenly. A hot hoosh was soon eaten and we plodded on towards a sharp ridge between two of the peaks already mentioned. By 11 a.m. we were almost at the crest. The slope had become precipitous and it was necessary to cut steps as we advanced. The adze proved an excellent instrument for this purpose, a blow sufficing to provide a foothold. I cut the last few steps and stood upon the razor-back, while the other men held the rope and waited for my news. The outlook was disappointing. I looked down a sheer precipice to a chaos of crumpled ice, 1500 ft. below. There was no way for us. The country to the east was a great snow expanse, sloping upwards for a distance of seven or eight miles to a height of over 4,000 ft. To the north it fell away steeply in glaciers into the bays, and to the south it was broken by huge outfalls from the inland ice-sheet. Our path lay between the glaciers and the outfalls, but first we had to descend the ridge on which we stood.

Cutting steps with the adze, we moved in a lateral direction around the base of a dolomite, which blocked our view to the north. The same precipice confronted us. Away to the north-east there appeared a snow-slope that might give a path to the lower country, and so we retraced our steps down the long slope that had taken us three hours to climb. We were at the bottom in an hour. We were now feeling the strain of such unaccustomed marching. We had done little walking since January and our muscles were out of tune. Skirting the base of the mountain above us, we came to a gigantic *bergschrund*, a mile and a half long and 1000 ft. deep. This tremendous gully, was semi-circular in form, and it ended in a gentle incline. We passed through it, under the towering precipice of ice, and at the far end we had another meal and a short rest. This was at 12.30 p.m. Half a pot of steaming Bovril warmed us up, and when we marched again, the ice-inclines at angles of 45 degrees did not look as formidable as before. Once more we started for the crest. After another weary climb we reached the top. The snow lay thinly on blue ice at the ridge, and we had to cut steps over the last fifty yards.

The same precipice lay below, and my eyes searched vainly for a way down. The hot sun had loosened the snow, which was in a treacherous condition, and we had to pick our way carefully. Looking back, we could see that a fog was rolling up behind us and meeting another fog that was coming up from the east. The creeping grey clouds were a warning that we must get down to lower levels before becoming enveloped.

The ridge was studded with peaks, which prevented us getting a clear view to the right or to the left, and I had to decide that our course lay back the way we had come. The afternoon was wearing on and the fog was rolling up ominously from the west. It was of the utmost importance for us to get down, into the next valley before dark. We were up 4,500 ft. and the night temperature at this elevation would be very low. We had no tent and no sleeping-bags, and our clothes had endured much rough usage and had weathered many storms during the last ten months. In the valley below us, we could see tussock-grass close to the shore, and if we could get there it might be possible to dig a hole in one of the lower snowbanks, line it with dry grass, and make ourselves fairly comfortable for the night. Back we went, and after a detour we reached the top of another ridge in the fading light. After a glance over it, I turned to the anxious faces of the two men behind and said, 'Come on, boys!' Within a minute they stood beside me on the ice-ridge. The surface fell away at a sharp incline in front of us, but it merged into a snow slope. We could not see the bottom owing to the mist and the bad light, and that the slope ended in a sheer wall occurred to us; but the fog creeping up behind allowed no time for hesitation. We descended slowly at first, cutting steps in the hard snow; then the surface became softer, indicating the gradient was less severe. There could be no turning back now, so we un-roped and slid down in the fashion of youthful days! When we stopped on a bank at the foot of the slope we found that we had descended at least 900 ft. in two or three minutes! We looked back and saw the grey fingers of the fog appearing on the ridge, as though reaching after intruders into untrodden wilds. But, we had escaped.

The country to the east was an ascending snow upland, dividing the glaciers of the north coast from the outfalls of the south. We had seen from the top that our course lay between two masses of crevasses, and we thought that the road ahead was clear. This, and the increasing cold made us abandon any idea of camping. We had another meal at 6 p.m. A little breeze made cooking difficult. Crean was the cook, and Worsley and I lay on the snow windward of the lamp, so to break the wind with our bodies. The meal over, we started up the long, gentle ascent. Night was upon us, and for an hour we plodded along in darkness, watching for signs of crevasses.

Then at about 8 p.m. – a glow which we had seen behind the jagged peaks resolved itself into a full moon, which rose ahead of us and made a silver pathway for our feet. We advanced in safety, with the shadows cast by the edges of crevasses showing black on either side of us.

Onwards and upwards through soft snow we marched, resting now and then on hard patches that glittered ahead in the silver light. By midnight we were again at an elevation of 4,000 ft. We were still following the light, for as the moon swung round to the north-east our path curved in that direction too. The friendly moon seemed to pilot our weary feet. We could have had no better guide.

Midnight found us approaching the edge of a great snow field, pierced by isolated nunataks which cast long shadows across the white expanse. A gentle slope to the north-east lured our all-too-willing feet in that direction. We thought at the base of the slope lay Stromness Bay. After we had descended 300 ft., a thin wind began to attack us. We had been on the march for over twenty hours, only halting for occasional meals. Wisps of cloud drove over the peaks to the southward, warning us that wind and snow were likely to come. After 1 a.m. we cut a pit in the snow, piled up loose snow around it, and started the Primus again. The hot food gave us another renewal of energy. Worsley and Crean sang their old songs as the Primus was going merrily. Laughter was in our hearts, though not on our parched and cracked lips.

We were up and away again within half an hour, still downward to the coast. We felt sure now we were above Stromness Bay. A dark object at the foot of the slope looked like Mutton Island, which lies off Husvik. I suppose our desires were giving wings to our fancies, for we pointed out various landmarks revealed by the vagrant light of the moon, whose friendly face was cloud-swept. Our high hopes were soon shattered. Crevasses warned us we were on another glacier, and soon we looked down to the seaward edge of the great ice-mass. I knew there was no glacier in Stromness and realized this must be Fortuna Glacier. The disappointment was severe. Back we turned and tramped up the glacier again, not retracing our steps but working at a tangent to the south-east. At 5 a.m. we were at the foot of the rocky spurs of the range. We were very tired. We decided to get down under the lee of a rock for rest. We placed our sticks and the adze on the snow, sat as close to one another as possible, and put our arms round each other. I thought that we might be able to keep warm and have half an hour's rest. Within a minute my two companions were fast asleep. It would be disastrous if we all slumbered together, for sleep under such conditions merges into death. After five minutes I shook them into consciousness, told them that they had slept for half an hour, and gave word for a fresh start. We were so stiff that for the first two or three hundred yards we marched with our knees bent. A jagged line of peaks with a gap like a broken tooth confronted us. This was the ridge that runs in a southerly direction from Fortuna Bay, and our course eastward to Stromness lay across it. A steep slope led up to the ridge and an icy wind burst through the gap.

We went through the gap at 6 a.m. If the farther slope proved impassable then our situation would have been desperate; but the worst was turning into the best for us. The twisted, wave-like rock-formations of Husvik Harbour appeared right ahead in the opening dawn. Without a word we shook hands with one another. Journey over! Though as a matter of fact twelve miles of country still had to be traversed. A gentle snow-slope descended towards a valley that separated our ridge from the hills behind Husvik, and, as we stood gazing, Worsley said, 'Boss, it looks too good to be true!' Down we went, checked presently by the sight of water, 2,500 ft. below. We could see little wave-ripples on the black beach, penguins strutting to and fro, and dark objects that looked like seals lolling on the sand. This was an eastern arm of Fortuna Bay, separated by the ridge we had seen below us during the night. The slope we were walking appeared to end in a precipice above this beach. But our spirits were not to be damped by difficulties on the last stage of the journey, and we camped cheerfully for breakfast.

Whilst Worsley and Crean were digging a hole for the lamp and the cooker, I climbed a ridge above us, cutting steps with the adze, in order to secure a view of the country below. At 6.30 a.m. I thought I heard the sound of a steam-whistle. I dared not be certain, but I knew men at the whaling-station would be called from their beds at that time. Descending to the camp I told the others, and in excitement we watched the chronometer for seven o'clock, for when the whalers would be summoned to work.

Eight to the minute the steam whistle came to us, borne clearly on the wind across the miles of rock and snow. Never had we heard sweeter music. It was the first sound created by an outside human agency since leaving Stromness Bay in December 1914. That whistle told us men were living near, that ships were ready, and that within a few hours we should be on our way back to Elephant Island to the rescue of the men waiting there! Our pain and ache, and our marches, belonged to the limbo of forgotten things, – and there remained only the contentment that comes from work accomplished.

From *South*, 1919

KATHERINE MANSFIELD

– Into the Bush –

I was hot and tired and full of discomfort – the buzzing of the mosquitoes – the slow breathing of the others – which seemed to weigh upon my brain for a moment, and then I found the air was alive with bird's song. From far and near they called and cried to each other. I got up, and slipped through the little tent opening onto the wet grass. The Caravan in the glade a ghost of itself – but across the clouded grey sky, the vivid streak of rose colour blazoned in the day. The grass was full of clover bloom. I caught up my dressing gown with both hands and wandered down to the river – the water downed on, musically laughing, and the green willows stirred by the breath of the dawning day, swung softly together. I forgot the tent and was happy.

Started walking into the bush, clematis and orchid. Meet Mary by the ploughed field and at last come to the Waipunga falls; then the fierce wind, the flax and manuka, the bad roads, camp by the river, and then up hill, the heat to Rangitaiki. Walk to post letters, camp on a peninsula – the purple, the ferns, the clean house – the shearing, the cream, the wild pigs. Woman and daughter, the man, their happiness.

From *Journal*, 1927

DORIS PILKINGTON GARIMARA

– Runaways of the Western Desert –

Molly, Daisy and Gracie tried not to look at the dark blue hills in the distance on their right. They were content to keep walking north at an easy pace that suited them well. Their sights were fixed on what lay before them. They had covered a lot of ground since crossing the main branch of the Moore River, over hills and sand dunes, and across the white sand plains. Yes, they were making good progress through the open banksia forests and they had covered a wide area of coastal, sandy heaths and had the pleasure of seeing a variety of flowers.

The girls were fascinated by the bright orange and white and red and yellow conical shaped banksia flowers. They pulled the branches down so that they could examine them more closely. Beneath the banksia trees, the ground was covered with a tangled undergrowth of plants, creepers, tufts of grass, decaying leaves and dry banksia nuts. It was almost impossible to find a patch of clean, white sand for them to pass through without scratching or stinging their legs on the prickly acacia bushes. Although it wasn't too bad when it was raining, because the cool drops washed and soothed the scratches on their skin.

They were almost past the clumps of banksia

trees when they heard heavy footfalls. It sounded like someone or something was heading their way. At that moment it began to sprinkle but they could still hear the footsteps. They were coming closer. There was a flash of lighting and in the distance there was a rumble of thunder. The footsteps were even closer.

'Quick', whispered Molly, and all three dived headfirst into the thicket and slid on their stomachs as flat and low as they could, not daring to breath. They kept very still, and waited for whatever it was to appear. Molly had no intention of being caught, sent back to the settlement, and punished by the authorities.

The footsteps were so close now that the ground was vibrating and they could feel every step it took. Then they saw it. The frightened girls couldn't believe their eyes, and they couldn't move if they wanted to. They could only lie and stare at the thing that was emerging from behind the banksia trees.

Grace started to say something in a low whisper but the words came out as an inaudible stutter. She gave up, and shut her eyes tightly and began to swallow deeply, trying to control her fear. For several minutes after the thing had gone by, its footsteps still thundering along, the girls remained on the prickly leaves, pondering whether or not it was safe to move. Their young hearts were thumping right up into their ears.

It was another few seconds before they regained their composure and their fear subsided. Only then could they rise and stand firmly on their feet, and continue their trek homewards.

'That was a marbu, indi Dgudu?', said Daisy, still shaken by what she had seen.

'Youay, it was a marbu alright . . . a proper marbu,' Molly added, shivering.

Yes, the thing fitted the description of the marbu, a sharp toothed, flesh-eating evil spirit that had been around since the Dreamtime. The old people always told children to be careful and to watch out for them, and now the three girls had finally seem one.

'The marbu had a funny head and long hair. He was a big one alright', said Daisy.

There seems to be only one explanation for that phenomenon, and that was the so-called marbu may have been a particularly large and hairy Aboriginal man with prominent facial features, who was running to beat the storm and the fast approaching nightfall. The man may have played on the girls' imagination and their belief in a mythical being of the Dreamtime stories. But to these children from the Western Desert it was genuine. And no one could tell them otherwise.

'Quickly', urged Molly. 'Let us get away from this place.'

From *Follow the Rabbit-Proof Fence*, 1996

Final Steps on Seven Continents

It has been a delightful journey, this journey home.
I have walked on foot.

– Olive Schreiner

JEAN-PAUL CLEBERT

– Lulled –

What a mute yet vibrant rebirth transforms this city – these streets, sidewalks, houses, lampposts, shady nooks, trees, urinals – once it is no longer covered, as with a skin, as with a crust, by people swarming larvae-like into the great machine of wage-labor – when, with night, it comes back to life, back to the surface, washing off its filth, straightening its back, scrubbing itself down, singing its silent song, lighting up its darkness. It stretches, relaxes, takes its ease, spreads out before me, the solitary walker, the stroller from elsewhere, free to explore its diverse extremities, thrilled to get lost in its labyrinthine immensity, turning at every corner, leaving a boulevard at the first street on the left, returning to the river, crossing it, tripping along, whistling softly with a cigarette butt between my lips. Darkest night. Three or four o'clock on a winter morning, the gas lamps on the backstreets are out, the trees in the parks carry on growing, the benches creak, vapor rises from the *vespasiennes* and the drain grids, a thousand million houses are just one house, an enormous flat barracks, covering kilometres as seen from the city's hilltops, the stones are cold, the cobbles gleam, and I settle by the curb of a square in a dry gutter, my eyes level with the street, and meditate, dream, forget to draw on my cigarette end, and, crossing my legs in the lotus position put my ear to the great seashell of the city, whose canopy covers and whose lowing . . . lulls me.

From *Paris Vagabond,*
translated by Donald Nicholson-Smith, 2016

ESLANDA GOODE ROBESON

– Never the High Grass –

Only a few yards ahead of us Papa lion went from the middle of the road to the high grass at the left edge, where he stood still for a second or two. Then Mamma lion came out of the grass beside the spot where Papa stood, followed immediately by an adorable baby cub. They crossed the road sedately, single file, with Papa falling in behind, then disappeared into the high grass on the right, and slowly walked away. We could see their tails just above the grass – held up stiff like flagpoles with the tuft of yellow hair at the end. Kaboha says they hold their tails erect when they sense danger. They were big tan-coloured animals with large heads and very thick shoulders, slimming down toward the tail; powerful looking but with a top-heavy, very unpleasant shape. Nyabongo says they always travel single file, the female first because she is quick and fierce and dangerous, the cub between for protection, and finally the male, which is slower, but sure and terrible.

I will never be able to walk in the high grass again. On through Katwe, round the Toro curves, home, – and gratefully to bed.

From *African Journey*, 1945

ALEXANDER KINGLAKE

– Own Armchair –

T hen begins your season of rest. The world about you is all your own, and there, where you will, you pitch your solitary tent; there is no living thing to dispute your choice.

My men, helped by the Arabs, busied themselves in pitching ours and kindling the fire. Whilst this was doing, I used to walk away, towards the East, confiding in the print of my foot as a guide for my return. Apart from the cheering voices of my attendants, I could better know and feel the loneliness of the Desert. The influence of such scenes, however, was not of a softening kind, but filled me with a sort of childish exultation in the self-sufficiency which enabled me to stand alone in the wideness of Asia – a short-lived pride, for wherever we wander, we still remain tethered by the chain that links us to our kind; and so when the night closed round me, I began to return – to return, as it were, to my own gate. Reaching at last some high ground, I could see, and see with delight, the fire of our small encampment; and when, at last, I regained the spot, it seemed a home had sprung up for me in the midst of these solitudes. The Arabs were busy with their bread – Mysseri was rattling the teacups – the little kettle with her odd, old-maidish looks, sat humming away old songs about home, and two or three yards from the fire my tent stood prim and tight with its open portal and welcoming look – a look like 'the own armchair' of our lyrist's 'sweet Lady Anne.'

From *Eothen*, 1844

FRANCES TROLLOPE

– Home Alive –

We had no sooner began to 'chew the cud' of the bitter fancy beguiling us in those mountain solitudes, than a new annoyance assailed us. A cloud of mosquitoes gathered round, and while each sharp proboscis sucked our blood, they teased us with their humming chorus, till we lost all patience, and started on our feet, pretty firmly resolved never to try the alfresco joys of an American forest again. The sun was now in its meridian splendour, but our path was short, and downhill, so again packing up our preparations for felicity, we started homeward. Or, more properly speaking, we started; for in looking for an agreeable spot in this dungeon forest, we had advanced so far from the verge of the hill that we had lost all traces of the precise spot where we had entered it. Nothing was to be seen but multitudes of tall, slender, melancholy stems, as like as peas, and standing within a foot of each other. The ground, as far as the eye could reach, was covered with an unvaried bed of dried leaves. No trace, no track, no trail, as Mr. Cooper would call it, gave us a hint of which way to turn; and having paused for a moment to meditate, we remembered that chance must decide for us at last. So we set forward, yes homeward, in no very good mood to encounter new misfortunes. We walked about a quarter of a mile, and coming to a steep descent, we thought ourselves extremely fortunate, and began to scramble down, nothing doubting that it was the same we had scrambled up. In truth, nothing could be more like, but, alas!, things that are like are not the same; when we had slipped and stumbled down to the edge of the wood, and were able to look beyond it, we saw no pretty cottage with the shadow of its beautiful acacias coming forward to meet us; all was different; and, what was worse, all was *distant* from the spot where we had hoped to be. We had come down the opposite side of the ridge, and now had to wind our weary way a distance of three miles round its base. I believe none of us shall ever forget that walk. The bright, glowing furnace-like heat of the atmosphere seems to scorch as I recall it. It was painful to tread, it was painful to breathe, it was painful to look round: every object glowed with the reflection of the fierce tyrant that glared upon us from above.

We got home alive, which agreeably surprised us; and when our parched tongues again found power of utterance, we promised each other faithfully never to propose any more parties of pleasure in the grim, store-like forests of Ohio.

From *Domestic Manners of the Americans,* 1832

146

WILLIAM BOYD

– This Was Rio –

I did this walk in the depths of Rio's winter. It was a cloudless day and the temperature was in the late 20s. The aim was to walk the length of the three famous beaches – Copacabana, Ipanema, and Leblon – which fringe the southern shore of the city, the most beautifully situated city in the world.

All public beaches are particularly democratic, but there's something about Rio's beaches that is almost revolutionarily libertarian. The beaches belong to the native denizens of the city, the cariocas, and they try to go there as often as possible: every day, if they can. The beach is part of their life – indivisible – and you sense this as you walk along it. On these beaches you encounter the city in all its astonishing variety: its cultures (sporty, commercial, illicit and narcissistic); it's people (black, brown and blue-eyed blond); it's hustle and bustle (the constant traffic of pedestrians, joggers, cyclists, and cars – there's a six lane highway that runs along the coast); its beauty (the wide, white beach, the enormous dotted vista of the ocean); its mundanity and tattiness (the 1960s high-rise apartments, the hawkers, the fishermen, the poor). The beaches are demarcated every kilometre by orange lifeguard stations, and the number of the station is what you tell your friends when you arrange a rendez-vous. Reputedly, number nine (on Ipanema beach) is where you see the most beautiful bodies and the smallest bikinis. If you're gay, check out number eight. Drink an *agua de coco* at the blue refreshment shacks; great cobbled green piles of coconuts signal a new delivery. Stop to watch the beach sport life: beach football, volleyball and, most extraordinary, the *futevolley* – volleyball played with the feet, head, and chest.

You leave Copacabana beach and cross the Arpoador headland to emerge at another long, curving vista. Ipanema and Leblon beaches stretch ahead. At the end, two green mountains rise: Dois Irmãos, the 'two brothers'. Your final destination is Leblon, which is more upscale with its bars and restaurants. Yet at the far end of Leblon beach on the hillside is a *favela,* the makeshift tin and concrete shacks clinging precariously to the near vertical rock face. The slum dwellers of the Leblon favela have one of the best views in Rio, looking down the length of Leblon and Ipanema. Time to rest in your tracks. This is Brazil.

From *Condé Nast Traveller*, 2006

EDITH M. RONNE

– Ushered to the Pole –

I t was bitterly cold! We noticed it at once, particularly on our faces. The chill factor was 80 degrees below 0, Fahrenheit, although the temperature was a mere minus 20. We marvelled at those who had made it the hard way. Never could we know the feeling of those intrepid men who had endured so much hardship and incredible sacrifice. For us it had been spectacular, and embarrassingly easy. Newcomers are ushered directly to the Pole, a few yards from the makeshift runway. We had just become the first husband and wife team to set foot there. I was the seventh woman to stand at the pole. The South Pole is about ten feet high and decorated like a barber pole. It is surrounded by the fluttering flags of the sixteen signatory nations to the 1959 Antarctic Treaty. The treaty 'froze' national claims and opened the Continent to science and peaceful purposes only. As we staved off frostbite, the photographers recorded my husband's presentation to Deep Freeze's commanding officer, Admiral Leo McCuddin, of two historic photographs, one of Amundsen in December 1911 and one of Scott a month later, both at the Pole. Then, hurriedly, we ducked into the entrance of our

Amundsen-Scott base and carefully descended the chiselledicystepstothebuildingsandtheirconnecting tunnels buried some twenty feet beneath the surface. Our stay at the base was concluded with a leisurely meal of steak, cafeteria style. The three-and-a-half-hour flight back to McMurdo (our main US staging area) was uneventful. But for me the day will remain forever the most memorable of my life.

From *Antarctica's First Lady: Memoirs of the First American Woman to Set Foot on the Antarctic Continent and Winter-Over*, 2004

– Forty Minutes for the Remains
of My Life –

I walk this exact route through my suburb of Flemington every morning. It's not beautiful or meaningful to anyone but me.

I barge out my front gate, under plane trees in which magpies sometimes warble. I cross the railway bridge, turn east at the house with the huge fig tree, then north again, past the brick garage and its inexplicably prolific gardenia bush. Nothing much to report till I reach the witch's house with the iron lace veranda and the hedge of dark pink rose bushes that no one's pruned for years. Every day I think their disgraceful neglect of those roses entitles me to pinch some on my way back. But I know I won't because my walk is a circle and I won't pass them again till tomorrow.

I cut through the booze warehouse car park and dash across the big road to the Bikram yoga school, then dive into the street with the weird antique shop on the corner. Good houses in a row, big wide Californian bungalows. Here, where the street drops downhill to the hockey fields and the concreted creek bed, I once saw a fox go strolling home at dawn. Another day a horrible man cursed me out and kicked my dog in the ribs.

Where the shared pedestrian and cycle track runs alongside the freeway wall I turn south again and pick up speed. Riders heading for the city zoom up behind me with sharp little warning chimes, and gusts of air as they pass. I'm breathing hard and feeling powerful. Here comes the old Chinese couple, the dead-faced woman and the husband with his desperate smile. A tradesman in hi-vis stands in the middle of the football oval, reaches for the sky and bows three times.

At the primary school I turn right and tackle the steepest hill. Halfway up, panting, nearly home, I cop the first lemony whiffs of my reward: pittosporum blossom. Its perfume floats between the houses from an invisible tree.

If I can scoop up that McDonald's rubbish from the playground gate and shove it into the bin without breaking stride, I'll have earned myself a lucky day. All this, with its seasonal variations, takes up 40 minutes of what remains of my life, in my undistinguished and beloved Melbourne suburb.

From the *Guardian*, 2018

– Globetrotting Gobbets –

I hope the pages turned have taken you for some good walks in the mind, have created some pictures and stirred some moods. Of course, footing it through the world can be caught in shorter accounts and here are seven to complete your reading journey – seven final snippets from the seven continents just covered.

Was I the German staying in Cáceres and walking around the world for a prize? They insisted that I must be German. That I must be walking for a prize. For what other reasons could a man walk.
– *V. S. Pritchett*

The weather in Luanda is undecided. And so am I.
– *Mary Kingsley*

He used to go to sleepwalking in Chumbi valley. His mode of progression was that of bending forward and it kept him going without any trouble. But he had one bad habit – he was a confirmed opium-smoker.
– *Francis Younghusband*

I could get more exercise. There is a path through the woods that I could take this rainy morning; but instead I will take the path to the pantry and mix a Martini.

– John Cheever

Walking across the plateau at Latacunga was where those giant volcanoes occupied my attention, and where I was rewarded with a magnificent eruption. And, I was abundantly satisfied!

– Ida Laura Pfeiffer

A beard in Antarctica seems to me as awkward and as unpractical as, well . . . let's say, walking with a tall hat on each foot.

– Roald Amundsen

One of Tasmania's beaches, a spit of white sand, stretching east to west, is named Bagehot Point, and it is a rare beach where you can walk into sunrise, and at the end of the day – into sunset.

– Nicholas Shakespeare

– Acknowledgements –

I shall borrow a word from the first traveller in these pages to say that a small 'Niagara' of people has helped with publication of *Globetrotting: Writers Walk the World*. It is my third book on walking for Notting Hill Editions (making up a loose trilogy), and at NHE all thanks go to – Rosalind Porter, Kim Kremer, Emma O'Bryen, Vera Sugar, Deborah Pike, and Robin Dennis. Elsewhere along the road, thanks are due to – Rachel Calder, Stephen McCrum, Emily Stubbs, Jonathan Morton, Clio Gould, Sophia Catchpole, Tim Giles, William Boyd, Helen Garner, and Michèle Roberts. And, finally, thanks to staff at the British Library, London, and to Woodbridge Library, Suffolk.

PERMISSIONS

Excerpt from *The Narrow Road to the Deep North* by Basho translated by Tim Chilcott. Translation copyright © 2004 by Tim Chilcott. Used by permission of Tim Chilcott (www.tclt.org.uk).

Excerpt from *Walking in Berlin* by Franz Hessel translated by Amanda DeMarco. Translation copyright © 2016 by Amanda DeMarco. Used by permission of MIT Press and Scribe Publications.

Excerpt from *Palestinian Walks* by Raja Shehadeh. Copyright © 2008 by Raja Shehadeh. Used by permission of Profile Books and Scribner, a division of Simon & Schuster.

Excerpt from 'St Olga' by Michèle Roberts from BBC Radio 3's *DuskWalks*. Copyright © 2010 by Michèle Roberts. Used by permission of the author.